I'LL GO

War,
Religion,
and Coming Home,
from Cairo to Kansas City

Alexs Thompson, PhD

Contents

Prologue: Afghanistan

"Get down!"

Lewis was yelling at me, his ordinarily polite South African accent twisted into a violent scream.

"What?" I was paralyzed. "Why?"

"I said get the fuck down!"

I took a quick glance out the window of the armored Toyota pickup truck and saw a man in a long white dress wearing a bulletproof vest about fifty yards away running toward us with a gun at his shoulder.

As I threw my head down against the leather seats, David, our American driver, gunned the engine toward the red metal gate that protected our house.

"Open the fucking gate!" Lewis screamed into his radio. "Open the fucking gate!"

We were stuck in the middle of downtown Kandahar between our office building and the safe house across the street. The gunman was on foot but had been closing in on us fast, and my mind was overwhelmed by what looked like the beginnings of an ambush.

When our Afghan security guards had barely opened the gate and let us in, Lewis started shouting again.

"Shut the gate! Shut the fucking gate!"

When the Afghans hesitated—I didn't know if it was incompetence or intentional—I heard, *pop-pop-pop*. The sound of gunfire whipped my head around and I saw a tall, slender figure collapse on the sidewalk.

Lewis saw it too but never stopped giving orders to everyone in earshot. He grabbed me by the shoulder and yelled, "Get to the safe room!"

I ran up the marble staircase into our ten-bedroom house, sprinted to the basement, and yanked open the metal door to the safe room. Once the last person on our team ran through the door, we bolted it closed and huddled on the floor.

Moments turned into minutes before my coworkers and I began to talk about how we would die. We could wind up like the aid workers down the street, shot by a terrorist who threw a ladder over the wall of their compound. Or a twisted mass of metal and flesh after our attackers threw a grenade in the room.

From the outside, the door to the safe room looked like part of the wall; there were no visible seams or handles that some terrorist could pry open to kill us all. That's what they'd told me when I arrived a few months earlier, anyway. But we all knew—everyone knew—that foreigners had safe rooms and they were always in the basement. Until that moment, we had all pretended that the safe room was actually safe.

"Did anyone see what happened?"

It was eerily quiet upstairs and people started wondering what was going on.

"Alexs, weren't you coming through the gate?"

"Yeah, but I'm not sure what happened; I just saw a guy running down the street and Lewis told me to get down."

Two hours passed before Lewis radioed down to say that the coast was clear and that we could go about the rest of our day.

I wasn't dead. I took a moment to let it sink in. When I slowly made it back upstairs, Lewis was surrounded and answering everyone's questions in the exact same way: "We're still figuring out what happened. I'll let you know when we get more information. Just trust me, we're all safe now."

I waited for everyone to disappear before I approached him.

"Can you talk?"

He grabbed me by the arm and pushed me into his room at the back of the house.

"She's dead, man."

My mind flashed back to the slender figure on the sidewalk.

Lewis slumped down in the chair next to his bed, suddenly deflated. I waited silently until he spoke in a hoarse whisper.

"Hossai."

"What! I just...I was just in her office! That's where I was coming from when I hopped in your truck. What happened?"

"She must have just come out of the office when the shots started."

I collapsed on the couch next to the door, asking myself over and over, *Is it worth it?*

I wondered if Hossai's life was worth it. It could have been me, not Hossai. Was this latest adventure worth my life? Was anything we were doing in Afghanistan worth the lives that were being lost? I was starting to lose the passion that had fueled my mission of chasing fundamentalists in the Middle East.

***

In 2010, I was working in Afghanistan for Development Alternatives International (DAI) as an economic development officer. After close to a decade of living in the Middle East, I believed that the true solution to terrorism was stable communities where people could earn an honest wage. Once people believed they could support their families, they wouldn't be tempted to support groups like al-Qaeda and the Taliban. I was in Afghanistan to help Afghans live the kind of life that we all want—free of violence.

DAI assigned me to Nawa District, a small enclave in Helmand Province in Southern Afghanistan. The Marine Corps had established a base of operations in the downtown market area, and I was supposed to design projects that would give people the courage to resist the Taliban. It was exactly the kind of work that I wanted to be doing, and I had the experience I needed to get the job done. I met with political leaders, teachers, and construction experts to figure out how we could rebuild schools, roads, and businesses. I had a $1 million budget for a district of less than 100,000 people, and when I landed, I was on a mission to change the world.

Eventually, though, it felt like I was just trying to buy my way out of a bloody war. Rather than doing what was right for the Afghans, it felt like the Marines, the other aid workers, the Afghans—and even me—were just trying to spend money so we could ask for more money. I couldn't figure out how to create real change. We had to march in single-file lines as we patrolled remote villages looking for terrorists. We had to work with Afghan leaders we knew were corrupt because we were worried they would help the Taliban attack us. Everything was meant to follow protocols, even if those protocols kept the same people making the same wrong decisions.

On the day of the attack, I wasn't even supposed to be in Kandahar. I should have been in Nawa, 100 miles away, building a road in Kandahar for Afghans who were struggling against the Taliban. I had spent weeks meeting with tribal and religious leaders trying to convince them that the Americans were there to help rebuild their society. Finally, they agreed to give me a shot by funding a road that would connect ten communities to hospitals, markets, and schools. The US Marines had declared Nawa a "priority district" because it was a breeding ground for the insurgency in Afghanistan, and this was my chance to make a real difference.

But there was a mistake in my paperwork, and I'd spent the afternoon going from the desk of one Afghan auditor to another, pleading for them to overlook the error. None of the people at my headquarters wanted to play ball. Rather than being helpful, they kept asking questions I didn't want to answer.

"Did you talk to Haroon? You know he's the chief auditor and the only one who can approve paperwork that isn't filled out correctly."

"Yes, but he won't sign my form. Can you talk to him for me?"

"I'm afraid there's nothing I can do, sir."

When I got to Hossai's office, I was frantic. "I'm begging you, Hossai. I told everyone in the community that I would get this road project approved."

Hossai was a young Afghan who was defiant in the face of the Taliban. Rather than heed their warnings that she quit working with foreigners, she proudly worked to help Afghans in her community. She was usually willing to help me if it meant we could accomplish our mission, but for some reason that day she was full of apologies.

"I'm sorry, sir, we have our regulations. If you look here, you can see that the community leader who requested the road project signed with his name on page 4; but on page 31, he signed with an 'X.' If he's literate, then we can't accept an 'X' as his signature. The rules for the government are very clear."

"Listen, Hossai, it's going to take me at least three weeks to get from here to Nawa. It will take a week to get on a military flight to Lashkar Gah. Then it's at least another week to get on a flight to Nawa and a few more days to convince the Marines to put me on a patrol that goes to the neighborhood where I'm working.

"And then I have to get back here to Kandahar, which could take another three weeks. It could be close to two months before I get back here for just one signature while the Afghans sit around and wait for a road to be built. Please help me with this."

"I'm sorry, sir, there's nothing I can do."

I stormed out of her office and into Lewis's truck.

***

I realized I was still on Lewis's couch incoherently muttering to myself, so I stood up and stumbled back to my room. I sat at my desk trying to figure out how I was going to help the people in Nawa, but I couldn't focus. When tapping on the keyboard didn't distract my mind enough, I pulled out a pad of paper and tried the physical act of writing.

It didn't work, so I jumped up.

I paced back and forth in my room, attempting to come up with a plan to trick one of the auditors into signing my paperwork, but my mind kept wandering back to Hossai. I wondered what I could have done differently. I wondered if she had left the office in a panic because I upset her. I wished I had kept talking to her longer. I worried that I had pushed her too hard to help me. I cursed myself for leaving Helmand and coming back to Kandahar before I checked my paperwork. I cursed God that I was in Afghanistan in the first place. And that she was dead and not me.

My mind tumbled backward uncontrollably until I found myself wondering how an abused, poor Black kid from Philly had wound up rewriting US policy in the Middle East.

Part One:
A New Kind
of Dream

Trouble at Home

My stepdad, Barry, was a violent alcoholic, but my mom had three kids from another man and nowhere to go but the bedroom of a tyrant. In many ways, it felt like I was raised to abandon my dreams before they were even dreamt. From the time I was three years old, it felt like Barry's only goal in life was to terrorize me and my two sisters. Even when he wasn't physically beating us, he would look at us as we passed him on the stairs as if to say, "I dare you to look at me wrong."

That's all it took, a wrong look. As a six-year-old, I didn't know what a "wrong" look was; I just knew that it meant I was going to wind up with bruises all over my body. A wrong look could turn a normal day of backyard barbecue into a torture session in the basement. I tried to look "right," but when that didn't work and the beatings kept coming, I just gave up. I pretended to look at him by tilting my head in his direction and slightly turning my body without actually looking him in the eye. If it had been up to me, I would have ignored him altogether, but it was disrespectful—another word I learned the hard way—not to look at someone who was speaking to you.

By the time I was seven, Barry had completely rewired my brain to act tough. I learned how to take care of myself, endure the pain, and fantasize about a different kind of life. By nature, I was a happy, curious child, but whenever I asked why clouds looked like violins, noticed that it never snowed in the summer, or chattered about the millions of questions that little boys ask their fathers, he destroyed my confidence.

One day, when I was eight, my parents had gone out to god knows where and left me and my two sisters alone. Makaela was eleven and Lakesha was six, and like most siblings we alternated between hating one another and being inseparable. After a dinner of baked beans and hotdogs, we came up with the idea of creating our own board game. Once we gathered up construction paper, scissors, crayons, and markers, we got to work pasting together the game board and cutting out the playing pieces. Just as we finished writing the rules on a piece of poster board, we heard our parents' car pull up in the driveway and got giddy.

"Mommy and Daddy are going to love it!"

My mom forced us to call Barry "daddy."

When they came up the stairs, we were beaming from ear to ear with the game board stretched out between us. Barry noticed the scraps of paper strewn across the floor and yelled at us. "What is this mess? We can't leave you alone for one night and you make a mess out of everything. Get your butts down to the basement right now!"

We lived in a row house on Basin Street in Norristown, a suburb of Philadelphia, and the basement was the only place where our neighbors couldn't clearly hear our screams.

When my stepdad came down the stairs, we were huddled together in expectation of the violence.

"Get over here!"

He called us forward one by one and swatted us over and over again with the extension cord from my boom box until our bodies were covered with welts. In the midst of that violence, as usual, he reassured us by saying, "You're lucky you didn't grow up with my father because he would strip us naked before he beat us!"

Lucky? If I hadn't been a scared little boy, I would have laughed.

It's not easy to act tough when you're an eight-year-old getting beaten with an extension cord or wire hanger for an hour, but I was tough in my mind. I feverishly resurrected the images of me and my sisters running around the house talking excitedly about the rules of the game and believing that our parents would be proud. I created a future reality where we finished creating our board game and all of our cousins came over to play and loved every minute. We took the game to school, won an award, and every kid in the neighborhood asked us to make one for them. I could almost feel the love that I craved so badly. Being able to create a new reality in the midst of pain became one of my most important abilities.

Eventually, Barry got too tired to beat us anymore—he probably came down from some high—and he threw the extension cord on the floor, stormed up the stairs, and went to bed. That was it. That was always it. There was a burst of unimaginable anger that just suddenly ended with three battered children trying to get on with their lives.

My two sisters and I held each other close on the basement floor until our brains could convince our bodies to ignore the pain and make our way to bed.

I lulled myself to sleep with extravagant stories about being reunited with my real dad: *He's not mean. He loves me. He's going to come find me one day. He's out there right now asking people if they've seen me and buying tickets to come get me and take me away.*

The next morning my mom woke us all up, yelling about the mess we had made and telling us to clean it before we could have breakfast. While we cleaned, Barry sat on the couch in the living room reading the Sunday paper and my mom cooked us a breakfast of pancakes, eggs, sausage, fried potatoes, and fresh-squeezed orange juice. We were expected to act like a normal family, and any sign of weakness from us was cause for another beating.

***

Finding my real dad, Alexs, was always the final scene in my imaginary life. Once that happened, everything would change. The beatings would stop; the yelling would stop. The pain would stop. I didn't know what came after that moment, but its imagined reality kept me acting tough.

I had only two memories of him: hailing a taxicab on the streets of Center City and laying in the bunk beds at his apartment in West Philly. He and my mom split up when I was three, so I didn't have any memories of what he looked like or how his voice sounded. I couldn't remember him and my mom together, him holding me, or any of the normal things that fathers and sons do.

Not remembering helped me because it meant I could make up any story I wanted. I created idyllic scenes in which my real dad patiently explained to me why clouds look like instruments and that snow is wintertime rain. Some days in the basement, I imagined he was a superhero with a big "A" scrawled on his chest, busy saving the world, and he would come back any day to rescue me. Or he was a brilliant scientist who was solving some crisis in a remote part of the globe and just needed a few more days to keep millions of people from dying. No matter what the fantasy, there was always a noble reason why my dad had left me to suffer at the hands of a monster.

My mom told me that he had abandoned us, but I never believed her. I knew that he was out there somewhere thinking about me and trying to find me. Every once in a while, I would screw up the courage to ask Aunt Margaret, my mom's sister, to tell me about him. The only things she would tell me was that he was from North Philly and was studying at Temple University when my mom met him. I guess my mom was immediately attracted to him, and he seduced her by taking her out to eat and to college parties. He was her ticket to a better life.

That's all I knew about my real dad: two memories that didn't add up to anything interesting and some stories from my aunt that made him seem like a manipulative jerk. Meanwhile, my stepdad constantly told me that my dad wasn't a real man because he had abandoned his family. The one thing everyone agreed on was that I looked like him.

By the time I was in middle school, I realized that I hadn't just gotten my name and looks from my real dad. I got my smarts and curiosity from him as well. When I was eleven and began writing short stories in my free time, I didn't know he was a professional writer and a successful businessman. I would learn over time that my dad and I were like twins separated at birth. In some ways, my mom and stepdad were right: I was just like my dad. I didn't share just a name and face with him; I shared his adventurous spirit of independence. They saw me growing to be more and more like my father the older I got, and they did everything they could to stop it. I sometimes thought my mom was scared that I would abandon her if Barry didn't destroy that part of me.

***

Barry didn't miss any opportunity to punish me for being myself. One day when I was thirteen, I came home from middle school beaming from ear to ear and clutching my report card. When I walked through the front door and into the dining room, I saw my mom in the backyard getting the grill ready for dinner and my stepdad sitting in the kitchen reading the paper.

"When is dinner going to be ready, woman?" he was yelling at her. "You're late already."

I pulled my report card out of my backpack just at the moment my mom walked into the kitchen and thrust it in her face with pride.

"We got our report cards today! I got mostly As and I get to take advanced geometry in eighth grade, which means I can take calculus in high school—"

I was talking a mile a minute.

My mom smiled weakly and seemed ready to congratulate me when my stepdad started in. "Don't come in here with that bullshit!" he yelled. "What? You think you're better than us? You're not better than anyone and you better get that through your thick skull. Those grades aren't gonna do you any good in the real world."

I'd heard all this before, but he continued, "All those white people are putting nonsense in your head, and they're not gonna be there when you need help. You better quit acting like them or you're gonna regret it."

I clutched my report card silently.

"Now, get out of here!"

Mom started banging pots and pans, and my stepdad snickered as I turned and walked out of the kitchen and stumbled back to my room in a state of confused defiance.

"You don't have common sense anyway!" Barry yelled after me.

I slumped down at my desk, cracked open my math book, grabbed my pencil, and started scribbling furiously in my notebook to erase the memory of that moment.

I didn't know what common sense was even though the phrase was thrown in my face almost every day.

"Those white people."

My parents told me all the time that I didn't act Black enough and that all white people were racists who could never love me.

I kept going back and forth between math questions and what Barry said until I crowded out his anger and memorized my geometry formulas. No one ever called me down for dinner that night, and I assumed it was my punishment for acting white. Given the other violent options, it was a punishment I took gladly.

God and Me

My two sisters were much better at pretending than I was. My older sister, Makaela, figured out how to be dumb. She was much smarter than me, but when Barry ridiculed her for getting good grades, she ignored her schoolwork; and when he laughed at her paintings, she threw away her brushes. She turned herself into someone that my stepdad could love.

It never dawned on me to stop writing short stories or getting good grades. I guess it's because they were the only things that made me feel good. No matter how badly he beat or ridiculed me, I was my only source of support. He forced me to work in his janitorial business and skip meals, but he couldn't break me. I tried to ignore my bruised body and conflicted mind and be a happy kid. I learned how to forget about the pain almost as soon as it stopped, and it drove Barry crazy. He found more ways to punish me: I wasn't invited when the family went on trips to Dorney Park or when the family gathered around for movie night with popcorn and candy.

Around the time of my fifteenth birthday, the tough act started to fail. I didn't know how to change who I was, and it started to kill me. The pain simmered under the surface until I found myself sitting on the corner of my bed tracing a razor blade across my wrists. I was having more and more trouble visualizing any kind of life but the terror of my current situation. The fantasy of a superhero father could no longer compete with memories from the basement.

No one loves you. Barry hates you. Your mom doesn't love you, or she wouldn't let you get beat all the time. Your real dad doesn't love you, or he would have saved you by now. You don't have any friends. No one loves you.

Love. It was another word I didn't understand. I heard my mom singing along with Whitney Houston and Anita Baker, but I never felt those feelings.

I started pushing harder across my wrist until I saw blood. It shocked me out of a dark haze. It was the middle of the night, but I yelled out loud, "No!"

Something inside me revolted against the growing sense of despair, and I refused to let it win. I don't know how or why, but I rushed to the bathroom and washed the blood away before putting a bandage on. I quickly peeked down the hallway to make sure no one could see me and I ran back to my room and lay down to sleep. In what seemed like a moment, I had created a new fantasy to lull myself to sleep.

No one loves me, but I don't care. I love myself. I will save myself. I will be my own superhero. I will save myself!

Even though I didn't know what it meant, those words kept tumbling out of my mouth and reassured me. I retreated into myself and focused on my new life where I wouldn't need anyone.

***

I don't know if my mom noticed the missing bandage or the faint scar on my wrist, but a few months later, she and Barry started going to church even though they had both grown up in the homes of abusive preachers. By the time we were all being carted off to church on Sunday mornings and Wednesday nights, I had already created my own personal salvation. I didn't know anything about Jesus or eternal damnation; I just knew that I needed to be my own rock in a world of pain.

At first, I didn't understand what was happening to my family. One minute we were being terrorized by my stepdad, and the next minute we were all sitting around the dining room table getting apologies for the years of abuse and hearing about the saving power of Jesus. We started going to Zion Hill Fire Baptized Holiness Church of God, where the old women fanned each other after they fainted during the three-hour Sunday services. The pastor was larger than life; he wore a long imperial robe with crosses stretched down either side that billowed with every word he boomed from his throne.

Church was explosive. There were people speaking foreign languages and dancing in the aisles while the drummer and organist stoked the flames of ecstasy. Our pastor taught that a true encounter with God whisked the worshipper from the physical reality into a spiritual reality where there was no pain, only a true connection with God. That grabbed my attention, and it didn't take long for the message of Jesus as Savior to change everything about my life.

I was sixteen, and it was a typical Sunday morning just before the excitement began; everyone was dutifully reading from their tattered Bibles as the pastor told stories about God's love.

"First John 4 and 16: And we have known and believed the love that God hath to us. God is love; and he that dwelleth in love dwelleth in God, and God in him."

Tears immediately welled up in my eyes. I didn't know why. Something clicked inside of me, and before I knew it, I was standing in the second row of pews with my hands raised and tears streaming down my face like everyone around me.

That's it. Love. Unconditional love.

I had heard the pastor quote that verse in casual conversation and sermons for months, but it finally hit me. I wasn't thinking about the last time I got beat or how alone I felt; I just had an outpouring of emotion. I wasn't fantasizing about becoming a famous mathematician or being accepted by my family; I was just experiencing a moment of love.

The drummer increased his tempo as the pastor shut his Bible, calling, "If you are suffering! If you have no home and no job! COME TO JESUS!"

He was leaning over the pulpit, pounding on the wooden platform in front of him with sweat and spit flying off his face. His robe was swaying back and forth as he ran from one side of the stage to the other, imploring us to reach out to the Lord.

"If you are downtrodden, discouraged, or afraid, RUN TO JESUS!"

His words shook me to the core.

"If you are suffering, find refuge in the Lamb of God!"

I knew he was talking to me, so I ran up and collapsed on the kneeler in front of the altar. I could feel the need for Jesus in my body. It didn't feel like any fantasy I had dreamed up in the basement; it felt real. As if Jesus was there with me, ready to transform everything about me and my life. To set me free from the real pain.

I didn't have any idea what was supposed to happen next, but I knew that my suffering had meaning because of Jesus. I wasn't suffering at the hands of a tyrant because I was a bad kid—it was just part of God's plan for my life. At that moment on the kneeler, Jesus became my personal savior. Not in the way the pastor talked about salvation and justification; it really meant the difference between living my life in my own way and death.

As my body convulsed in prayer, I relinquished all of my fantasies to Jesus. I wiped away the images of my real dad, and I displaced myself from the center of an imaginary universe. Jesus was the right mix of superhero and victim to help me survive my reality. I knelt there, actually believing the Holy Spirit would descend on me as he'd descended on the Apostles on the Day of Pentecost.

And then I felt a hand on my shoulder. I was snatched away from my new reality by Barry, who had come down the aisle after me and was pulling me to my feet. He whispered, "God will give you what you need."

I looked at him with tears streaming from my eyes, yearning for acceptance, and he looked back with embarrassment. I was making a spectacle of myself, and he wanted me to get myself together.

Dreaming a New Dream

Barry stopped drinking, swearing, and doing drugs, but the mental abuse worsened. I was still never good enough at the things he and my mom cared about and too good at the things they didn't care about. Thanks to that Sunday morning experience, though, I only cared about Jesus. The pastor's sermons were riddled with analogies to fatherhood, the good son, and the value of suffering. Everything from church reinforced what had always seemed to be true in my heart: I wasn't a bad person, and I deserved to be loved. I learned to dream a dream that couldn't be taken away from me.

I did everything the pastor said. I read my Bible every day, prayed unceasingly, became a witness for Christ, and practiced forgiveness against my enemies. Especially Barry. Those disciplines brought an unknown peace to my life and convinced me to become a pastor. When I graduated from high school in 1993, I enrolled at Eastern College, about 10 miles from home, to study youth ministry so I could share the story of Jesus with kids who were suffering. I scored high enough on the SAT to get scholarship and loan money to afford college on my own—and get out of that house forever. Or, at least, I thought so.

On the first day of freshman orientation, I was at the head of the pack with our tour leader as she shepherded us around campus, pointing out the important buildings nestled between brightly colored trees and the ponds with wooden bridges over them. Most of the other new students were looking around nervously and avoiding eye contact with everyone else, but I felt like a caged beast that had been set free. My home had been a prison cell where I had learned about suffering, patience, and finally God's redeeming love. Going to college was my chance to share that message with the world, and I was excited to talk to anyone who would listen.

"Hey, what's your name?"

One of the other students tapped me on the shoulder. I looked up to see a beaming smile on a big, broad-shouldered white guy wearing jeans and a flannel shirt.

"Alexs. What's yours?"

"Bret. Where're you from?"

"Norristown. It's just about twenty minutes from here. How about you?"

"I'm from Shamokin; it's about two hours from here."

"Oh, cool. What made you come to school here?"

"I don't know, really; it seemed like a good place to go. Maybe I'll become a missionary or an artist. I'm not sure. How about you?"

Bret and I kept chatting away as the tour guide walked us through the chapel and across campus to the college auditorium.

"I want to be a youth minister," I told him. "I want to preach the Gospel to kids going through the worst periods of their lives."

Bret was over six feet tall, and without warning, he reached out and pulled me into a massive bear hug. "I knew there was something about you," he said. "I saw you and I just thought to myself that you have a good spirit. You're going to be a great youth pastor someday. I know it."

No one had ever talked to me like that. I had never heard anyone talk to anyone like that.

Bret let me go and asked another question. "So, you're going to major in youth ministry?"

"Well, I'm going to major in youth ministry and math."

"Really?" Bret was laughing.

"Yeah. I know I want to help kids, but maybe God wants me to do that by teaching or becoming a pastor. I learned French in high school—maybe I'll do that. I love Jesus, and I'll do whatever He wants me to do."

"That's how I feel, Alexs. God has blessed me with the gifts of an artist and I don't know what to do with them. I won a scholarship to the School for the Arts, and when I was there they said that I was one of the most gifted painters they had ever seen. Maybe God wants me to be an artist."

"I believe that God will make our paths clear, Bret. Do you?"

He hesitated for a moment, surprised at my direct question. "I do."

Soon after Bret and I started talking about our lives, the tour ended, and then we were sitting in my dorm room chatting nonstop. We talked like that all night. We walked back across campus to the dining hall for dinner and prayed in the chapel on our way back to my room. When bedtime rolled around, we were already best friends.

***

Freshman year was exactly what I had hoped it would be. All of my professors recognized me as one of the smartest people in my classes and went out of their way to encourage me. My biology professor urged me to apply for an internship in the summer, and Duffy Robins, my youth ministry professor, took me with him to local speaking engagements so I could learn what it was like to work at a church. Most importantly, I finally felt that there were people in my life who accepted me for me.

Bret and I spent all of our time together and shared everything. My first roommate left school after a few weeks, and Bret slept in my room most nights. We kept the keys to his car in my room and took whatever cash we needed from a jar that sat on my desk—Bret got money from his family, and I worked odd jobs. I felt closer to Bret than anyone I had ever known, even my parents and siblings. Sometimes I felt closer to him than I did to God—he was the closest friend I'd ever had, and the life we shared helped chip away at the walls I had built up as a kid.

I was living the life I'd dreamed of as a child.

Then my real dad called the phone in my dorm hallway.

A few months earlier, my older sister, Makaela, had found one of his poems in an anthology and had written to him. He wrote her back, and they began repairing their relationship one letter at a time. Whenever I went home for the weekend, she told me how good things were going and that he wanted to call me. After reading some of the letters he wrote, I agreed to talk to him on the phone.

"Hey, son, how are you?"

"Fine."

"Oh, ummm, that's good to hear. What's the weather like in Philly?"

"I'm not in Philly. I'm at Eastern College in St. Davids."

"Oh…that's right," he said. "Well, how are your classes going, I mean…what classes are you taking?"

"Theology, biology, calculus, and some other stuff."

I talked to my dad with the steely disaffection of a teenager who was pretending to be something he wasn't. I knew I should want to talk to him, but I didn't know how I was supposed to act. So I acted tough, as if our relationship didn't mean the world to me, as if he wasn't the culmination of my earliest fantasies. My dad was clumsy in his questions, and it was obvious that he didn't know what he was doing. He lacked the confidence I needed from him. He didn't have an explanation for why he had abandoned us. He just kept erupting with questions until I couldn't handle it anymore.

"How is your family?"

That was the question that did it for me. I didn't think about it; I just hung up the phone, walked back into my dorm room, and started throwing books around the room. I tried to sit at my desk and do my biology homework, but the scratching of the pencil against the pages of my notebook didn't help calm my nerves. His voice sounded like mine, and it was unbearable. I worried that all the other things people said about him were true. Maybe I was being disloyal to my mom and stepdad.

My emotions became uncontrollable, and I broke everything within reach.

After a while, there was a knock at the door and Bret walked in quickly, grabbed me, and took me to the chapel. He must have heard the commotion and waited until it subsided. He prayed with me, and then we started walking around campus.

"I don't know why I hung up." I could barely talk above a whisper.

"Maybe you shouldn't talk to him anymore."

Neither of us knew what we were doing or how to solve this new problem, so we just walked around in silence before we went to bed.

My dad kept calling, and I kept hanging up midway through our conversations. Even though I wasn't sure if we could ever create a relationship, I kept answering the phone. The more we talked, the more my anger was replaced with curiosity at the reawakening of a dream I had buried under the story of Jesus. A few months later, when he told me he was coming to Philly to visit his mom and sister, I agreed to have dinner. I still didn't know what it meant to have a relationship with him, but I could finally think about trying.

We agreed to meet on the edge of campus. I was standing at the top of a long set of stairs down a steep incline to the road, and when he got out of his rental car, I stopped and stared. When I made it to the bottom and he opened his arms for an embrace, I realized that he was shorter than me and had dreadlocks that hung down to his shoulder. He was moving toward me as slowly as I was, and we eventually met in the awkward embrace of two strangers who were supposed to love one another. He smiled weakly at me and fell back on familiar questions to fill the uncomfortable silence.

"Hey, how are you?"

"Fine."

He took me to an Italian restaurant near campus that served fancy food on white tablecloths. He broke the silence shortly after we sat down, asking, "Do you drink?"

"No."

"Do you mind if I have a drink?"

"I guess not."

We went on like that as we looked over the menu, but I slowly started to see more of myself in my dad.

"I'll have the spaghetti with meatballs, but no cheese."

My dad ordered exactly what I was planning to order, so I changed mine to chicken parmesan with no cheese.

It was unavoidable. The more his face stared back at mine, the more I saw myself and heard my voice. It was an exciting realization, but without thinking, halfway through my chicken, I asked the question I didn't know was gnawing at my insides.

"So, what happened between you and my mom?"

"Well. That's a tough question. I guess we just grew apart."

"No, I mean, what happened? How did you get separated?"

"What do you mean?"

"I mean…what happened?"

"Don't you know what happened?"

"No."

My dad got uncomfortable. And ashamed.

"This isn't easy."

He hesitated and took a long drink.

I pushed my chicken around my plate, watching him gather his nerves.

"We were living in that small apartment in West Philly trying to figure out how to be adults, but we were fighting a lot. We didn't know what we were doing. But we had you three kids, so we didn't want to talk about what it all meant. I was trying to start a career and move on with my life and she…well…"

I could tell the subject still hurt him.

"We just didn't know what to do…"

I didn't try to help him out by asking questions or telling him it was okay.

"…and then I got an interview for an advertising job in Minneapolis. A very good job making a lot of money…"

The pauses only amplified the pain in his eyes and in my heart. "When I got back from the interview, you kids were gone. You, your sisters, your mom. You were all gone…and then I packed my bags and moved to Minneapolis."

Every urge in my body told me to flip over the table and storm out. For a moment, there was only emotion. Inwardly, I yelled to myself, *It can't be true. None of that can be true.*

I said slowly to my dad, "My mom always told me that you abandoned us."

Everything became jumbled in my mind. *Was my mom wrong? Was my dad lying? He could have called us or written to us.*

"Look, Alexs. I'm not going to make excuses, and I'm not going to blame anyone but myself. Yes, she took you kids away from me, but I didn't go after you. I ran away because I was afraid. I fucked up. There are no two ways about it. I can't change the past, but I can change the future…I can change the right now. I just want to create a new relationship with you. You can ask me whatever you want, and I'll tell you the truth."

I didn't ask him any more questions right away.

We sat there in silence, clanking our forks and knives against our plates, until I started to feel people around the room looking at us and I asked him, "Why are those people staring at us?"

I nodded toward the people two tables over, expecting him to get angry and tell me that they were racists who didn't like Black people being in the restaurant. His answer changed the entire course of our relationship.

"Don't people stare at you all the time? Don't you find that strangers pick you out of a crowd and talk to you? They tell you about their life without you asking them?"

I sat there, stunned, and my dad just smiled at me. He was right. Bret had rushed through a crowd of people to introduce himself to me and share his life. He had never met a Black person before, but he was drawn to me for some reason that he could never fully explain. Things like that happened to me all the time in college, but I figured it was the light of Jesus shining through me. I assumed it was proof that God was proud of me.

"Well?" My dad was waiting for an answer.

"How did you know that?" I asked.

"Because it happens to me all the time."

We spent the rest of the night talking like reunited friends. "What about your love life?" he asked as we made our way back to campus.

"My only love life is with God until I get married."

My father didn't know all the things that had happened to me as a child or understand why I was talking about God when he was asking about girls. The more we talked, though, the more I understood that he was a critical component of the new life I was building.

Saint Francis

I was excited to meet my real dad, but from the moment he dropped me off at the dorm that night, I felt a growing sense of confusion. It became unbearable to think about who I could have grown up to be—I couldn't even put words to the swirl of thoughts that clouded my brain. Above all, I found myself questioning the death grip I had on the Lord: Should I drop out of school and move to Minneapolis? Was Jesus the only way for me to build a new life? Or could I create the kind of life I dreamed about with my dad? It was as if my dad had swooped in in the dead of night and reawakened hopes and dreams that had been buried on that kneeler. Two of my most powerful fantasies were clashing with one another.

My confusion was resolved when I found myself lying facedown, alone, in a small Methodist church outside Eau Claire, Wisconsin, imploring the Lord for guidance. Bret and I had driven to our friend Jim's house for spring break to go four-wheeling, shoot guns, and distract me from my thoughts. Jim's dad was the pastor of a small church, and when I closed the door behind me, I reenacted the scene from a verse that I had been reciting over and over for months.

Ezra praised the Lord, the great God; and all the people lifted their hands and responded, amen, amen. Then they bowed down and worshiped the Lord with their faces to the ground. (Nehemiah 8:6)

I prayed with everything I had. *I only need you, God. I only need you, God. You are my salvation, but I feel distant from you. I need Your love to continue on, but I don't feel You like I used to. I don't want to doubt Your plan for my life, but I don't know what to do.*

As I lay there with my arms spread out and my head dug into the plush red carpet, I heard a voice say, "Saint Francis."

The voice repeated itself before I had the courage to look up.

"Saint Francis."

It yelled at me, "Saint Francis!"

I hopped to my feet and looked around. The voice implored me.

"Saint Francis!"

Seeing no one, I fell to my knees in fear. The voice boomed one last time before everything went silent.

Saint Francis.

I believed in the Holy Spirit and that God talks to people, but I didn't believe it could happen to me. I thought I must have temporarily gone crazy. I wasn't even sure I understood what I had heard. After a few moments of silent confusion, I turned off the lights and ran from the church to Jim's spare bedroom, where I sat shaking with uncertainty. I rifled through my backpack, pulled out a book on prayer, and found Saint Francis of Assisi listed in the index. As I pored over the text, I learned that Saint Francis was rebellious young man whose father wanted him to run the family business in medieval Italy. After years of carousing with friends, Francis grew tired of the party life and became obsessed with being knighted; when war broke out with a neighboring region, he rushed to the frontlines. Soon after he went to war, though, he was captured and spent a year as a prisoner of war before his father paid the ransom.

Legend says that while he was a prisoner, he started receiving visions from God, and by the time he returned from war, he refused to follow in his father's footsteps. He spent most of his time alone in the countryside, and after months of fighting, Francis's father became exasperated and dragged him to the local magistrate for punishment. Rather than submit to the demands of his father, Francis defied everything that was expected of him, stripped naked in the town square, and stormed off into the woods, where he built a community of selfless religious penitents that eventually spread throughout the world. I was instantly inspired by a man who had abandoned everything the world told him he was supposed to do and followed God's plan for his life.

I immediately dedicated my life to Saint Francis and, just as quickly, pushed my dad to the back of my life. It was a drastic decision, but more important than anyone or anything was my commitment to myself. Francis found freedom when he completely rejected the world, and I needed to do the same thing. The first time I felt free was on that kneeler at Zion Hill Fire Baptized Holiness Church of God because I was completely removed—in my mind—from a painful reality. I wasn't just mimicking what the Psalmists complained about; I was actually being beaten regularly to the point of having welts, bruises, and broken bones. The pain of the Psalms was really my pain, and I experienced true freedom when I could create my reality and define my own future. When Barry pulled me away from that kneeler, it wasn't the first or last time that someone tried to tie me down to their reality. Saint Francis became the most important role model in my life because he helped me understand that I needed to run away from the real world—naked, if necessary—when it crushed my ability to be the hero of my life's story.

By the time I was in college, I was already fueled by a deep sense of being unloved; Francis let me shroud that discomfort in idealized religious principles. The story of Jesus defined the principles of the life I wanted to live, and Saint Francis—by stripping himself of worldly expectations—showed me how to live that life. In a lot of ways, my origin story was similar to his: when Saint Francis found me, I was already obsessed with the modern version of the knight in shining armor—the superhero. What I didn't know was that my independent spirit would drive me to war just like his spirit did him.

By the time we got back to Eastern College, all I could talk about was Saint Francis, and I made a beeline to the local Catholic church to talk to the priest. Father Peter was happy to talk to a local boy from the Baptist college because it was a way for him to stick it to the Protestants. He wasn't just smart—he knew the Bible better than any of my professors and could translate from Latin and Greek—and he understood the passion that had driven Saint Francis to strut through his hometown in his birthday suit. Priests, like Saint Francis, had to give up everything to serve God, and I became fascinated with the Catholic religion. Rather than just explaining doctrine, Father Peter challenged me to experience what Francis must have felt.

"Jump in!"

We were on one of our regular walks in the woods near Eastern College when he surprised me with this command.

"What?"

"Jump in the creek. Just do it."

Father Peter wasn't yelling, but he was stern. I talked nonstop about how much Francis was consumed by an uncontrollable love for God, and Father Peter challenged me to feel what it must be like to completely let go.

"I can't just jump in the creek. I didn't bring a change of clothes."

I had never been a spontaneous person. I learned to measure everything before I said it, and I didn't put myself in situations where I couldn't predict how everyone would react.

"Saint Francis preached to birds and rabbits. Don't you think he would have jumped in a creek?"

"…Probably," I admitted reluctantly.

When it became clear that I wasn't going to jump in, Father Peter put his arm around me and laughed. "Jesus loves you. And I love you, Alexs."

We stared at each other for a moment before he broke the silence.

"But don't worry; I wouldn't jump in that creek, either."

We both laughed.

"You have passion in a different way, Alexs. You follow your heart, and that's a special thing."

It wasn't easy to leave the Protestant church, but I began to believe that Saint Francis had visited me in Wisconsin to define the next stage of my spiritual journey. Even though most of my friends argued against it, I went through the conversion process, and in spring 1996, I was welcomed into the Catholic Church. I took Francis as my confirmation name.

***

While I was deciding to join the Catholic Church, Bret started to wonder whether he should drop out of school and join the military. The more we talked, the more the military seemed like a great way for both of us to live our passions, and we eventually decided to join the Navy. I talked about how Saint Francis had gone to war and Bret thought about how much money his brother had made when he enlisted. At the appointed hour to sign our contract, though, Bret said he had a last-minute paper to finish and I went by myself. Although I kept asking, Bret never signed up for the Navy. On the last day of school, before we left for summer break, he asked me, "What are you going to do?"

"I'll go and see what it's like. What do you think?"

"I think it will be fine."

"Do you think you'll do it?"

"I'm not sure."

We stared at each other until he broke the silence by saying, "I love you, Alexs."

I was afraid to go off to the Navy by myself, but the example of Saint Francis inspired me to keep reaching out into my new reality.

"I love you too, Bret."

The next week, I was sitting in my parent's house, waiting for the Navy recruiter to take me to boot camp. When I joined the Navy, I was looking for an adventure, but besides being poked and yelled at for hours at a time, life as a sailor was little more than an extended workout session. I signed up to be a Machinist's Mate and spent my days learning about how ships are designed and maintained, yet I couldn't muster any enthusiasm for the work. I got to travel, made more money than I ever imagined, and made good friends, but I started to lose sight of the life Saint Francis had inspired me to live. Halfway through my four-year enlistment, I found a medieval-style monastery in Virginia where I could live out my obsession with Saint Francis. As in all my other adventures, when I had free time from the Navy, I didn't go home or see my friends. I went to a monastery where the monks lived silent lives of manual labor and Gregorian chanting.

I remember one of the first times I retreated from the Navy and visited the monks. We were chanting Matins, the 3:00 a.m. prayer service that is almost entirely composed of reading the Psalms. I had been so excited to get my day started that I set my alarm for 2:00 a.m. and snuck my way into the choir stall of the main church before anyone else had awakened. When the brothers started to shuffle in, shaking off their deep sleep, I picked up my prayer book and concentrated every part of my body on the words on the page. The brother on my right, Paul, was equally intent on the pages in front of him, even though he had been praying the same Psalms for forty years. Father Thomas, on my left, closed his eyes, hung his head, and mumbled his way through the prayers as if he was barely interested. Standing in the choir stall was like hiding inside a voluntary prison cell. Everyone had their own style, but all of the brothers and priests were focused on one thing: replacing everyday life with a total focus on Jesus. That commitment tempted me to give away all of my possessions and join the monastery. I felt free to just be myself in the darkness and silence of the monastery praying the Psalms in a completely new way than I had at Zion Hill Fire Baptized Holiness Church of God.

Mornings started so early that I didn't have time to think about Navy life, and my afternoons were spent working and studying with Father James. It was a perfectly peaceful way to separate myself from the world and live my passion. It took two years of going back and forth from the Navy to the monastery for me to realize I couldn't become a monk. Saint Francis didn't just hide away in a cave and devote his life to God; he traveled around Italy and abroad, inspiring people to live better lives by his example. I decided to do the same thing.

In my last week at the monastery, I told my spiritual adviser, Father James, that I couldn't spend the rest of my life there. He had been my personal priest, given me an education in monasticism, and heard my daily confession. It was a difficult conversation for both of us. I felt that I was walking away from something that had fundamentally changed who I was without knowing where my life was headed. Once again, I was on the run, but I didn't know where I was going. Or what I was running from.

Father James didn't say goodbye until I was standing outside waiting for Brother Benedict to bring the car around so we could go to the airport. Suddenly, I felt a hand grab me by the elbow; I dropped my seabag and spun around to see James staring at the ground. He stammered, "Hey."

I knew immediately that something was different because he usually greeted me with "Good morning, Mr. Thompson," or "You were late for Mass, Mr. Thompson." He never said, "Hey."

"How are you, Father?"

"I really enjoyed learning with you, Alexs. I hope you'll come back, even if it's just for a visit."

He started talking before I knew what was going on, and then he took a step closer. As he reached in for a hug, he said, barely above a whisper, "I love you."

I stood there in shock as we hugged. I had grown fond of him, but I never expected him to show me anything but fatherly guidance. He had always been kind and committed to helping me learn, but he had never given me any indication that he thought of me as anything other than a curious kid who dropped in and out of the monastery. When he released me from his hug, he turned around quickly and made his way back to the dormitory.

***

I decided to leave the Navy around the same time I abandoned the monastery. I had been in the Navy for four years and I was still listless, searching for something I couldn't put into words. I moved into my mom and stepdad's new home in Exton, another suburb of Philadelphia. I hated the thought of living with Barry again, but I didn't have any other options.

It wasn't the first time—or the last—that I would reinvent myself. As with every other transition, I immediately set my goals: finish college, get a job, and plan for my future. It took me two weeks to get accepted to Pennsylvania State University and find a job at the local YMCA as a lifeguard and swim instructor. One day, a month after I had started working and studying full-time, I was walking around the neighborhood to clear my head when I noticed a volunteer fire station. I didn't think twice; I walked up to the wide bay doors and introduced myself to the first person I met.

"Hey, my name is Alexs."

"How's it going?"

Pawsy was a big fireman who was irritated I was interrupting his afternoon of sitting on the front ramp and staring off into nowhere, but I wasn't deterred. In the few moments it took me to walk up to the station, I knew that being a fireman was the next phase of my passion-filled life.

"Good. I just moved into the neighborhood. What do I have to do to join?"

Pawsy looked me up and down.

"The monthly meeting is tonight. Come by around seven."

That completed our conversation. He got up and disappeared somewhere into the station, and I turned around and continued my walk.

Within a few days, I was accepted into the Lionville Fire Department and was issued firefighting gear. We had a few training sessions from time to time, but most of my training happened on the road. I learned how to cut people out of cars with cutters and spreaders, called the "jaws of life," and put out fires by watching the guys next to me. When my pager went off, I raced out of my house and ran up the street to hop on whichever truck was about to roll out of the station.

The adrenaline rush was addicting. We ran car wrecks on the Pennsylvania Turnpike and small fires in the neighborhoods near the station. Most of the firemen didn't have much else going on in their lives, so we spent our Friday nights out at dinner, drinking beer at the station and running calls. They became my new family. We had absolutely nothing in common except for the fact that we were lost souls who were willing to run into burning buildings and rappel off the side of busy roads. Within a few months, I was spending all of my free time with them, whiling my life away at the station and getting drunk on the weekends.

***

When I wasn't at the fire station or working at the YMCA, I was studying. At Penn State, I took classes on religion and politics and discovered that Saint Francis was revered in other religions as a holy man. The more I read about how famous he was around the world, the more I started reading about meditation and the great mystics from other religions. My studies opened me up to the reality that there were other religions that preached a life of total surrender to God, and I became enamored with Buddhism.

I remember sitting in a political science class, watching a documentary about the genocide in Rwanda and wondering whether prayer and meditation could have prevented that violence. That question started to burn inside me, and I walked out of class knowing what I wanted to do with my life: bring meditation to international politics. By that point in my life, I always followed my passion. Whether it was living in a monastery, fighting fires, or planning my future, when I felt passion burning inside me, I ran in whatever direction it pointed. I didn't need to know where it would lead, only that it was an expression of my purpose in life.

In the fall semester of my senior year, I started looking for graduate schools to study religion and found the perfect program at Naropa University in Boulder, Colorado. Naropa was founded as a Buddhist school and emphasized spiritual development as part of its academic program. That meant that in addition to my courses in religious history, they would teach me meditation. Then I saw the price tag. Even with the maximum amount of financial aid, it would have been tens of thousands of dollars in loans, and I didn't want to go into debt.

After the initial disappointment set in, I discovered Naropa was just down the street from the University of Colorado at Boulder, which also had a master's degree in religion. I was accepted to both schools for fall 2001, and the choice was easy because CU-Boulder gave me a teaching assistantship, which paid my tuition as well as a salary. As soon as I finished reading my acceptance letter, I rushed off to show it to my mom and Barry. They were unsurprisingly disinterested. Barry barely looked up from his paper, and my mom took a momentary pause from setting the table for dinner. I ran up to the fire station and found that Pawsy was the only person there. When I told him my good news, his reaction wasn't much better. "You're not going anywhere! You're gonna be stuck here like the rest of us."

He sounded mad.

"Screw you, Pawsy, I'm getting outta here."

I sat there next to Pawsy, fuming and waiting for the next fire or car accident. I couldn't believe he had said that, but it struck a chord in my heart. I had spent most of my time with Pawsy and the boys at the fire station for almost a year. They were my closest friends, and I told them everything about my life. Slowly, I realized that the adrenaline of pounding on the chests of dead people was an expression of the burning passion inside me. I wasn't born to be a fireman; I was born to do whatever it took to live out the boundless energy that animated me. Fighting fires was just one of the ways I would do that over the course of my life, and Pawsy was just another person who tried to keep me from living life on my own terms. As I counted the minutes until I could hang my head out of a fire truck barreling down the highway, I didn't realize I was weeks away from the adventure that would define the rest of my life.

Part Two: A Middle East Adventure

Chicago

T wo weeks after I landed in Boulder, the Twin Towers were destroyed.

It was my first semester of graduate school and I hopped out of bed to the sound of someone banging on my door. I was pissed off until I saw my roommate breathing and pointing erratically. "Did you see what they did?"

"Who?"

He didn't respond but turned and started running. We bounded up the stairs to the living room and stood there as the first tower collapsed. The reporters were trying to calculate how many people were in there. Hundreds? Thousands? My head started spinning, and I collapsed on the couch while the second tower fell. We just sat there in silence until we couldn't take any more of the commentary.

I kept asking myself, over and over, "Who did this? Who are they?"

I couldn't imagine who could be capable of such a horrible act. None of my readings about Sinn Féin or the genocide in Rwanda helped me make sense of those two buildings falling to the ground. After the initial shock wore off, I managed to get myself ready for school. My first class of the day was with my adviser, and I could only stare at him blankly as he taught us about the earliest religious movements in America. It had only been two hours since I watched those horrid images, and I was still unable to put words to my emotions.

As soon as class ended, he pulled me aside. "I noticed that you seemed distracted during class. Did you see what happened in New York?"

"Uhhh…yessir." I had been out of the Navy for over a year, but I still referred to everyone as sir and ma'am.

"Are you okay?"

"I…I'm fine."

"Are you sure?"

"Yes. Yes. I'm fine, thank you."

On my way home, I sat down on one of the benches in Norlin Quadrangle and started scribbling in my notebook. I needed to find a way to express what I was feeling, but the words escaped me. Eventually, I was just tracing circles over and over until I had a flash of revelation. I didn't know where it came from, but it was clear and inspiring. *This is exactly why you're studying religion!*

The voice was as real as anything that had ever happened in my life, and I knew I had to map out a new future. When I wrote my application to CU-Boulder, I had said that I wanted to use the principles of meditation to help prevent international conflicts, and now I had a specific mission. I rushed home and turned on the TV. The more I watched the news, the more I learned who they were: the people my roommate and I knew nothing about were Muslims from the Middle East.

By the next day, I had devoted my life to studying Islam, and all I could talk about was the Middle East. Within a week I was carrying an Arabic language book everywhere I went and started looking for schools where I could get a PhD in Islam since CU-Boulder didn't have one. In that week I had changed course and redefined the direction of my life.

Then, Dr. Marvin Wilde, a world-renowned scholar from the University of Chicago, came to CU-Boulder early in my second semester to talk about the role of religion in the 9/11 attacks. Listening to him fundamentally changed my life. After his lecture, Dr. Wilde met up with professors and graduate students for dinner at Rincon del Sol on the north side of campus, and it just so happened that we sat next to each other. Once we found out we were both from the suburbs of Philly, we really hit it off and I told him I had written a paper a few weeks before that made some of the same points as his lecture. When I told him I'd learned French in high school, we bantered back and forth about the differences between the conjugations of verbs and his favorite restaurants in Paris. Eventually, I realized that he was asking me more and more difficult questions about current events and anthropological theory. When we parted ways, he told me he had enjoyed getting to know me and asked me to email him my paper.

The next morning, after the haze of alcohol and excitement of speaking French dissipated, I started to wonder whether I might have made a connection with Marvin. It reminded me of what my dad had told me in that Italian restaurant when we first met: "Don't you find that strangers pick you out of a crowd and talk to you?"

Maybe it wasn't an accident that Marvin had sat next to me.

The next Monday, I went to the office of Bill Welk, the professor who had arranged for Marvin to come to campus, thanked him for arranging the lecture, and told him I had had a great time talking with Dr. Wilde at the bar.

"More importantly, Mr. Graduate Student," Bill asked, "what did you think about his lecture?"

I laughed. "Yes, sir! Actually, I really liked what he talked about. I just wrote a paper that argued something similar, and I sent it to him."

Bill was trying to remind me that I should have been more interested in the lecture than the free booze. He and I got along pretty well because he was from Pennsylvania, and he helped me adjust to how academics talked. Both of us had grown up poor and had never thought about graduate school, but Marvin Wilde had taken Bill under his wing and helped him adjust to the academic lifestyle.

"Have a seat. I need to tell you something," Bill said, getting serious.

I collapsed dramatically on the couch just inside his office. "Okay, Doctor, what is it?"

I was piling on the drama because I thought Bill was going to tell me that I had stepped over the line between graduate students and professors.

"Marvin wants you to study with him in the Divinity School at the University of Chicago."

Bill let me sit there and take it in. I needed a long moment to process the magnitude of a famous scholar asking me to study at one of the best schools in the world.

"Me?"

"Yeah." Bill chuckled at my astonishment. "He said that he was really impressed with the way your mind works."

I sat there for another moment. Then I started laughing. I couldn't believe this was true. But Bill wasn't laughing. After a few more seconds, I hopped up and asked him what I needed to do to submit my application.

**

The University of Chicago was the best place in the world to study religion.

And Islam.

Almost all of the professors in the religious studies department at CU-Boulder had their PhDs from the University of Chicago, and most of the books we read in class were written by people who had graduated from there. Marvin's invitation was all the more shocking because I hadn't even considered applying—I assumed I would never get in. I had always thought it was like getting into NASA or winning the Fields Medal—I just didn't have a chance.

It took me a few weeks to get my transcripts, recommendations, and writing samples together, but Bill helped me through the entire process. While I waited to hear back about my application, the reality of an acceptance letter started to hit me. A PhD from the University of Chicago was a golden ticket; I would be able to get a job teaching at any university I wanted. Or I could get a job in Washington, D.C., writing Middle Eastern policy. I didn't know what I would become, but I knew that if things worked out, I would be a totally different person. When I finally got that big package with the Divinity School seal in the upper left-hand corner, I started screaming and yelling at the top of my lungs. I didn't mean to be so caught up in the moment, but I felt free. Like I could do anything and go anywhere. I was going to live out my wildest dreams.

I called everyone. My mom and stepdad didn't care, so I called my dad and he got it. "Wow! That's fantastic news, Alexs. That's a great school. How did you manage that? I didn't know you were applying to PhD programs."

I was too excited to be cool and my words were tumbling over each other. "It's not a PhD program. It's a master's degree because I won't graduate from CU-Boulder, but when I do the master's at Chicago, there's a 90 percent chance they'll accept me into the PhD program."

"This is really good news, Alexs. I'm really proud of you…oh! I know someone who has a kid in Chicago. Let me put you in touch with her."

"I almost forgot to tell you! They gave me a full scholarship and a $10,000 stipend!"

"What?!"

"Yeah, they said I was one of the most qualified students who applied."

The conversation was short and we wound up talking over each other for the most part, but he was the first person who understood the magnitude of me going to such a famous school.

***

My first trip to the University of Chicago was for Prospective Student Day. When I landed at Midway Airport in the spring of 2002, I made my way to the baggage pickup, through the parking garage, and out to the bus terminal and took the 55th Street bus to Hyde Park—the home of the University of Chicago. I glued my nose to the window during the forty-five-minute bus ride, watching the neighborhood signs go from Spanish to English. Even though I had already been accepted, I grew more nervous, and I was knocked back in my seat when we pulled up to the campus. It looked like Oxford or Cambridge, with ivy climbing up its walls. The homeless people were gone and the streets surrounding the university were vibrant with patches of grass as wide as soccer fields between the lanes. I was immediately hooked. Despite the weeks that I had known Marvin

Wilde and fantasized about going to the University of Chicago, it didn't feel real until I hopped off that bus.

I met my potential host family on Saturday, and we immediately hit it off. They were a young Black couple who had both just finished medical school. Amos had gotten his MD from the University of Chicago and was finishing his PhD in biology. Lesia had gotten her degree from Midwestern University and was doing her residency. She was tall, beautiful, and devoted to her family. They had two young children, and everything about my new house was completely different than anything I had known as a child.

By the time I went back to Boulder on Sunday, I knew I was beginning my new life. The dean, Wendy Fowler, told me that there weren't any students in the Divinity School studying Islam and she would do whatever she could to help me succeed. It took her only a few days to secure additional funding for me to attend an intensive program in Arabic before my first year. The long days would allow me to complete a year's worth of language study in one summer, and by August 2002, I was sitting in my first class at the University of Chicago, paging through my Arabic textbook and waiting for our instructor to show up. The dusty old classroom with wooden desk chairs from the 1950s reminded me of a classroom scene from the Indiana Jones movie *Raiders of the Lost Ark*.

When the instructor, Ahmad, walked into the room, he didn't say a word before he started scribbling on the chalkboard. I had been studying the Arabic alphabet, so I could make out some of the letters, but I didn't have any idea what they meant. Ahmad, a graduate teaching assistant, finished writing, turned to us, and opened with a dramatic reading of the words on the chalkboard. He first recited them in Arabic several times, which none of us could understand, and then translated them into English.

Arabic is a key to a room with no other entrance or exit. Inside that room is nothing but a closet. The closet has a large imposing door with a solid ivory handle and golden trim. Inside that closet is an ornate wooden chest with golden etchings of buildings from across the known world. Inside that chest is a small metal box that blinds whoever gazes directly upon it. Inside that box is nothing.

I bellowed. I laughed so loudly that my head rocked backward, and I grabbed my belly because it felt so good. Ahmad had told that story in a way that made each of us eager to hear what was in the box, pausing at certain points and elongating his words at others to draw us into his short story. Post-9/11, every part of the government was clamoring for people who knew Arabic, and there were jobs at universities all over the world for scholars of Islam. I didn't know exactly what to do with my Arabic skills, but I knew there were so many opportunities to make a real difference.

When Ahmad began talking about the room and the closet and the door, I imagined that this was my first exposure to Arabic wisdom and ancient truths that would hold the key to understanding why terrorists had blown up the Twin Towers. This would be the knowledge needed to help shape US foreign policy or design college courses that would equip future diplomats and soldiers. And so I had expected Ahmad to say that the box contained happiness or serenity or something profound. And then he dropped the punch line. When Ahmad told us that there was nothing in the box, I didn't believe him.

Arabic summer school was eight hours a day, with at least three hours of homework each night. I assumed that we were all going to need some powerful incentive to keep up our motivation, and Ahmad was trying to get us talking about what learning Arabic really meant to us. As I rocked in my seat, I guessed that Ahmad's little joke could actually be a great icebreaker for a class of twenty people who were going to be spending a lot of time together.

But Ahmad wasn't joking.

I hadn't noticed that no one else was laughing. As I unclasped my hands from my belly and opened my eyes, I saw a few sneering faces and contorted bodies turning to see the guy causing all the trouble in the back. This was one of those moments when it would have been great to have Bill Welk remind me that graduate students at one of the premier universities in the world don't burst out into laughter on the first day of class. I propped myself up in my chair, opened my book, and buried my nose as far into the vocabulary list as possible.

My fellow graduate school students, unfortunately, weren't as excited as I was, so day after tedious day, I trudged down the muggy streets of Chicago. I dragged my Arabic books from my new house to class, or to a restaurant or bar, and back home again to do my homework. I sat in that classroom with people who never talked about 9/11, and I became distracted by the normal patterns of everyday life: who was sleeping with whom, who had gotten too drunk over the weekend to study, and who thought they were definitely going to fail out of class. Like most of them, I was struggling so hard to learn a new religion, culture, and language that I could barely keep up. It was the first time in my life that I was pushed to my intellectual limits. Everyone at the University of Chicago was smart, but Arabic seemed impossible for all of us.

When fall semester began, classes were equally as difficult and it motivated me to reach out to my real dad more and more. He had started teaching at local colleges in Minneapolis and was the kind of sympathetic ear I needed to navigate the new world of academia. He understood not only the anthropological theories I was studying but also the difficulties of fitting in with other graduate students. The more we talked, the more he started visiting me in Chicago, and the dynamics of our relationship naturally changed. He helped me so much with my studies that I didn't have to think about him anymore as the realization of childhood fantasies. Instead, I reengaged him as someone who could help me get better grades. The more we talked about school, the more we were able to talk about life and build a deeper connection.

One weekend, he was staying at the House of Blues Hotel in the Loop, and when he answered the knock on this door, he found me standing outside, reading the newspaper. I walked in, saying, "I'll just finish up this article real quick."

"Yeah, okay, I'm just watching a little TV."

When I lay down on his bed, I remembered something I'd wanted to ask him. I put my newspaper down and looked in his direction just as he walked over to the CD player sitting on the dresser and started talking to me at the same moment I started talking to him. He began, "You know, I wanted to see if you've heard this…"

Then we asked the same question at the same time: "Have you heard of Musiq Soulchild?"

We stood still for a moment, staring at each other. Not only had we recently discovered the same artist, but we'd thought about it at the same time.

There was a long silence.

Without realizing it, we had become comfortable with each other. That moment revealed a connection that had been lingering in the background that neither of us had been ready to admit. It was unplanned, and it changed the way we thought about each other forever: we finally realized that we were connected in a way that could never be broken. We both laughed and started going through the album song by song. We stopped trying to figure out how to be father and son and learned to be best friends.

***

Living with Lesia and Amos also had an unmistakable impact on how I imagined my life. They doted on their two children, Amos, Jr., and Mary, and it was the first time I saw a properly functioning family. When Lesia and Amos had a disagreement, they went up to their bedroom and didn't come down until they'd resolved it. When one of the kids got in trouble, they weren't taken to the basement; their parents sat them down on the couch or the back steps of the house and explained their mistake. Lesia and Amos disagreed plenty, such as what to have for dinner or how to discipline Mary when she broke Amos's favorite watch, but there was never any destructive violence.

Living with them was the kind of therapy I needed to put my own home life in perspective. Amos introduced me to conscious hip-hop music and opened my mind to a whole new way of thinking. My stepdad had always ridiculed me for acting white, and that shame had stuck with me. I was ashamed to be smart because only white people were smart. I was embarrassed that I loved to smile and was uncontrollably curious. My skin felt uncomfortable, so I ignored it. I had been programmed to believe that every bad thing about me stemmed from not being Black enough. There was always a fundamental difference between how I thought about myself and how I assumed everyone else thought about me. The combination of studying human behavior in graduate school and living with Lesia and Amos forced me to think about how my body was defined by myself and others.

People were always telling me, "Well, you're not like other Black guys. You're…you're just different." There were words that people used to describe Black men who weren't Black enough or man enough, and at some point all of them had been used on me.

Soft. Oreo. Faggot. Wannabe. Pussy. They all meant one thing: different.

At one and the same time, it meant nothing and everything. Even though I was able to compartmentalize what other people thought, those words haunted my subconscious. I knew that I'd never had a long-term girlfriend, but I never figured out how to care enough to go about getting one. Even with Barry, I knew that if I just got worse grades, was less curious, and did as I was told, everything would be better. But I just couldn't force myself to make changes that didn't resonate with who I felt I was. I could only ever be true to myself—no matter how painful it was. Somehow, it all revolved around sex and skin color. I felt like an outcast because I didn't act like a normal Black man. It was a really fucked-up way of thinking, but it was handed down to me through song lyrics, music videos, movies, and—most importantly—Barry. The reality of normal, everyday life, that I struggled so mightily against, suffocated me.

Thanks to Amos, my mindset was transformed by a conscious hip-hop artist from the Bronx named KRS-One. In his song "Brown Skin Woman," he yells at the listener to recognize that their skin is not black. I looked at my left arm and was shocked to see brown skin. I had never thought about my body in any way other than how I had been taught. I was a Black man. It seemed embarrassing, but I had never thought about the difference between my skin color and the color black, but in a moment, it explained the discomfort I had with how I had been defined throughout my life. And once again, I made an instantaneous decision: I declared that I no longer identified as Black, male, or straight. It was just the kind of extreme reaction I needed to reject a reality that had weighed so heavily on me.

My behavior didn't change. I didn't start wearing women's clothing, sleeping with men, or being white. I wasn't trying to change who I was; I was trying to force people to accept me for who I had always known myself to be, to change the way I let people talk about my body. The more I rejected those terms, the freer I felt. More free than I could have ever imagined by rejecting three little words. It was exactly what KRS-One said: he wasn't screaming at his audience to intimidate them but to protect himself from a world that tried to force its labels on him.

Chicago became a laboratory for me to start living out a new life, and I needed to find a new way to learn Arabic. After studying it for six months, I still had no idea what was going on in the Middle East, and I couldn't conjugate the most basic verbs. The 9/11 attack had lit a fire in my belly that wouldn't let me take my time. I had to do something to make the world right again. By January 2003, I started to think that the only way for me to learn Arabic would be to go to the Middle East, and I floated the idea to another student.

"You haven't been studying Arabic long enough. Why don't you give it some time?"

"I'm already in second-year Arabic and can barely read a news-paper. It's frustrating as hell."

"Second year?" She laughed. "Alexs, it's going to take four years before you can even read a newspaper, much less be fluent in Arabic. And that's if you're lucky. Just be patient and take your time. Have you taken a class with Ahmad yet? He's really good."

"Oh. Okay, thanks."

I didn't have time to argue about why I needed a faster way to study Arabic.

Nothing in that language made sense to me: the letters looked completely different than English, there were at least ten sounds in Arabic that did not exist in English, it was written from right to left, and it didn't always show short vowels or punctuation.

'nd 't dsn't 'lwas show shrt vwls 'r pnctuatn

In English, it would be like reading *shrt* and not knowing whether it referred to "shirt" or "short." Or *pt*, which could be "pat," "Pat," "pit," "pet," "put," "pot," "opt," or "apt."

The list of things I didn't know piled up during those endless hours of homework and made me feel stupid. It pissed me off, and in March 2003, without much preparation, I packed my bags and started my next adventure.

Cairo

It was pitch black outside as we made our final turn toward the terminal. The darkness receded from the runway lights and the familiar buzz of buses and shuttles set my mind at ease. I was on solid ground after a fourteen-hour journey, and I pressed my face against the window trying to accept the fact that I was on the other side of the world. As the flight attendant squawked away on the intercom, I started making out the writing on the airport:

"Al..."

I tilted my head to make sense out of the Arabic calligraphy sprawled across the length of the terminal in front of me. The first part was easy; Ahmad taught us on the first day that *al* meant "the," but I felt like I should have been able to translate more than one word after two years' worth of Arabic lessons.

I tilted my head the other way and squinted my eyes but couldn't make sense of the squiggles dancing along the entire side of the airport terminal. The fact that I was having so much trouble convinced me that my last-minute decision to go to the Middle East in the middle of an undeclared war was the right thing to do.

"Al-kaaaaaww…"

"Al-kaaawheera…Al-Qahira…"

After some effort, I finally read my first word in Arabic in an Arab country.

Al-Qaahira! Cairo.

I was in Cairo and I had read the Arabic word for Cairo. It felt like conquering Mount Kilimanjaro. It was a simple task, but for the first time since I had left the Philly suburbs, I was doing something; I was making my way up the mountain of Arabic.

The flight attendant was giving the same instructions I'd heard on planes around the world, except this time they were in Arabic and English. I was filled with energy and conviction as I got up from my seat and grabbed my bags from the overhead bin. It wasn't until I started making my way to the front of the airplane that I remembered I had absolutely no idea what I was doing.

I had traded six emails with a man named Abu Ali who ran an Arabic-language institute in Egypt, near Cairo but not in Cairo, which had no physical address, a fly-by-night webpage, and no affiliation with any American institution. All of my classmates who had gone to the American University in Cairo were shocked that I was going to a place no one knew about. I picked Abu Ali's school because I didn't want to do what everyone else had done. I wanted a real Egyptian experience.

As the front of the plane came into view, it dawned on me that I had absolutely no idea what a real Egyptian experience was.

Abu Ali had told me that I would be picked up at the airport, but I had no other details. I didn't have any contact information except an email. There was no phone number I could call or any physical description of the person picking me up. Problems I hadn't considered began to loom large in my mind when I saw the jetway.

What if no one picks me up?

What if the wrong person picks me up? Even if they are the right person, will they speak English?

In my hasty departure, it had never dawned on me to ask how I would communicate with my family and friends or whether there was Internet where…wherever I was going,

I had never asked him where I would be staying.

In just a few steps, I grew terrified of the reality unfolding before me.

I pretended that I knew what I was doing as I made my way through immigration. When they spoke to me in Egyptian Arabic, I paid attention to their hand motions and eye movements to figure out what they meant. I kept my passport in plain sight so they could point to it or grab it when they needed to. After being stamped and waved past all the necessary checkpoints, I pieced together what words I could read as I moved past immigration—*mukhrij* meant "exit," so I followed those signs. I reached the outside.

It felt sticky and dark.

There were a few taxis lingering around, waiting to pick up a passenger for a fare, but most of the people on my flight had already been picked up by their relatives or drivers. After a few moments, a man slowly approached me. He didn't smile and he didn't speak English. I could tell he was trying to utter the words "American" and "Alexander," so I smiled broadly to break the tension and showed him my passport. He grabbed my bag and walked off toward the parking lot as I blindly followed him. As we approached his car, a woman emerged from the front seat and quickly moved to the back seat.

She was covered all in black. Hands, face, feet, everything. There was nothing visible. The only time I had ever seen a woman dressed like that was on TV, and it was usually with people who celebrated the fall of the Twin Towers. Time began to slow down, and I could feel my breathing get shallower and quicker. My legs grew heavy and my feet felt like they were growing roots into the asphalt parking lot. I looked left and right to scan for any other people who might be able to help me, and I yelled internally at myself, *Getting into a strange car in a strange land with a man who doesn't speak English and forces his wife to wear that thing is a bad idea, an idea of epically bad proportions.*

I just kept moving, fueled by senseless passion. I opened the passenger door slowly and sat down while reaching for the seatbelt as if I were going out partying with my buddies back home. My body was moving in slow motion but my mind was spinning in circles. The driver hopped in the car and took off like a bat out of hell. We sped along darkened roads at breakneck speed. I was surprised to notice we were on a four-lane highway with light posts, dotted lines, and shrubs for decoration. It looked more like the long, uninhabited road out of Denver International Airport than whatever I expected Cairo to look like. All three of us sat in silence as I tried to get myself together and plan for whatever was going to happen to me.

I lost track of the time, and when we finally pulled over and stopped in a residential area, I was exhausted. I had expected to see the wildest creatures I had read about in fairy tales, but I was greeted by sights that were more normal than foreign. I remember walking through a dense residential area with four-story buildings, up some flights of stairs, and into an empty apartment. The driver dropped my bag in the living room and left as I collapsed on the closest bed.

***

The next morning, I woke up coughing and wheezing, but I re-assured myself, *I'm not dead. I'm really in Egypt, and I'm not dead.*

I sat up slowly on the bed and surveyed my body and belongings. I reached into my pants pocket to make sure my passport and wallet were still there, then got up and pushed on all the windows and doors to make sure they would open.

When I realized I wasn't a prisoner, I waited for the phone to ring or someone to knock on the door. I began to explore the entire apartment, which had three bedrooms, each furnished with queen-size beds, large wooden dressers, and small desks with chairs. There was no one else in the apartment and nothing to indicate that someone would be appearing anytime soon. One of the rooms had a window that looked out onto the street below, but my room and the other room just faced an enclosed courtyard.

Two hours turned into three hours, and my fear faded into the background. It didn't disappear; it just became part of my environment. I didn't need to *feel* afraid because I *was* afraid. I needed to expend my mental energy, figuring out what my next move was and not obsessing about the worst possible thing that could happen. Eventually, I sat in front of the window that looked down onto the street. There were way too many women covered from head to toe in all black, but there were also kids kicking balls down the street, men on bikes selling everything from books to water, and donkeys carrying carts. I sat there observing the world below me for another hour before I made my way to the living room.

There was a large wooden china closet with glass windows and no dishes on the shelves or silverware in the drawers, a couch on the left side of the door, and a dining room table with chairs to the right. As I walked closer to the table, I noticed that it had a large doily mat and a piece of paper on it with scribbles. The apartment was completely empty, so finding a scrap of paper with scribbles on it felt like I had won the ultimate prize. I assumed the now-familiar position of squinting and twisting to make sense of the Arabic letters.

Is…

Isk…

Iskandar.

Alexander. It was a note addressed to me.

I stared and squinted. I tilted my head one way and then the other. I could read the signature: Muhammad. Anyone who studies Arabic sees the word *Muhammad* a hundred times a day because it is the name of the Prophet and a common name in the Arab world. Nothing else made sense, so I read and reread the word *Muhammad*.

As I fingered the small slip of paper, I figured that it must be a note left by the driver. I walked back to my room, where I was surrounded by my things, and sat down on the bed. The note was too short to be directions. I knew I wouldn't be able to figure out every word, so I tried my hardest to pick out words here and there. The only thing I cared about in that moment was how to communicate with the language institute.

If it wasn't directions, then maybe there was a phone number or an address. It was a short handwritten note, so I reconfigured my brain to look for numbers. I found a string of numbers and sprinted toward the phone in the kitchen, hoping I didn't need to know an area code. It rang once before a person answered. "Aywah."

I responded quickly, "Yes, hello, this is Alexs Thompson. I'm in the apartment. Can you come get me?"

I stopped, wondering, *What does* Aywah *mean?*

I hadn't flipped the right switch. I was so relieved to find a phone number and actually connect with a human being that I hadn't prepared my brain to speak and comprehend Arabic. So I took a quick second to switch modes and translate *Aywah*.

Nothing.

Months of Arabic classes, and I had no idea how to initiate a phone conversation.

He repeated his greeting: "Aywah…man ma'ee?"

This guy on the other side of the line was speaking to me in Egyptian Arabic, and I had no idea what he was saying. I only knew the medieval-sounding Modern Standard Arabic, and I wasn't sure he would understand me.

Switching to a different mode, I resurrected three words in Modern Standard Arabic that most people would understand: "Ana issmee Iskandar." (My name is Alexander.)

I spoke that phrase loudly and slowly, fully aware that I sounded like an idiot. I knew it was grammatically correct, but it had to be wrong in Egyptian Arabic.

"Ahhhhh, Iskander, 'Amal eh?"

The voice on the other end of the line strung together sentences of Egyptian that meant nothing to me. I could tell he understood my name, and I hoped he knew where I was staying. There was some shuffling of the phone and a brief silence before someone else got on the phone.

"Is this Alexander?"

A tremendous sense of relief washed over me. The person on the phone was speaking English! It was British English, but by god, someone was speaking English to me.

"Yes, it is; who is this?"

"This is Yusuf. Someone will be over in a few minutes to bring you to the Institute."

And then the line went dead.

How long was a few minutes? Who was this Brit I had just spoken with?

I sat down on the couch and waited. My brain was starting to function properly, but I was still in survival mode. I hadn't showered because it hadn't dawned on me to do so. I hadn't eaten, but I still wasn't hungry. I was fighting jet lag but couldn't feel the fatigue. I just wanted to get on with the adventure.

As I sat there jittering with excitement, waiting for Yusuf or Muhammad or whoever from the Institute to come get me, I laughed at my poor planning. I could have easily gotten an international phone or SIM card before I left Chicago. I could have plugged the name of the school into Google Maps and gotten an idea of how far it was from Cairo and learned some important Egyptian phrases. But I hadn't done any of that.

Fifteen insufferable minutes later, there was a knock on the door, and it was Muhammad. I didn't mean to, but I hugged him and started babbling in Arabic, "Salaam alaykum! Kayf al-hal?" (Hello! How are you?)

I smiled and smacked him on the back and shook his hand vigorously, and he was surprised by the sudden eruption of emotion. I had no idea who Muhammad was, but he was a familiar face and he was going to take me to Yusuf, who spoke English. Muhammad smiled weakly, returned my greeting in Arabic, and pointed me out the door of the apartment.

I followed him down the stairs and began taking mental notes on how to navigate back to my new home. Everything was different.

It didn't feel like a prison anymore. If they wanted to kill me, they probably would have done so already.

Down two flights of stairs, turn right, down a long street.

Past one apartment building. Two apartment buildings.

A store with Arabic letters and an old man sitting on the front stoop.

Another store with Arabic letters and the word *Shop* scrawled underneath in English. Halfway down the block, I noticed an Internet café and tried to hide my excitement that I had found a way to communicate with the outside world.

The main road was a four-lane divided highway, probably the same road that we had taken from the airport. No more than fifty feet down the main road on the left was the Institute—a converted house with a big banner on the front. There was no fence, just shrubs separating the building from the road, and the same type of shrubs lined the walkway from the main street to the actual building. As I took time to survey my surroundings, Muhammad stood at the doorway of the Institute, beckoning me to come in.

A voice suddenly spoke to me in English, "Alexander, how are you?"

Oh, thank god, I thought to myself.

It was the same voice that I had heard on the phone. I turned to see Yusuf emerging from behind a curtain at the back of the building. I was about to tell him the funny story about my journey and how I had woken up in a panic, but I stopped when I noticed he was wearing a traditional Islamic long-flowing white garment called a thobe. In some ways, it reminded me of the robe worn by my pastor at Zion Hill Fire Baptized Holiness Church of God.

"I'm good. How are you? Are you Yusuf?"

I was dressed in khaki pants and a button-down short-sleeve shirt. It was hot in Cairo. Very hot. I wore pants because I didn't like wearing shorts, no matter how hot it was outside. Apparently, Yusuf didn't like shorts either. He looked Pakistani British, but he was wearing sandals, and his crisp, white thobe went down to just above his ankles. He had a small breast pocket on the left side and some kind of ID and a roll of cash tucked inside. I didn't know exactly what to think about a British guy wearing Islamic religious garb, but I figured I should keep my mouth shut.

"Would you like some tea?"

Yusuf was serious, but I had an almost uncontrollable urge to laugh. *It's a bazillion degrees outside, dude,* I said to myself. *Why would I drink hot tea?*

"Yes, please."

Yusuf disappeared behind the curtain as I sat down on one of the chairs in the lobby. It was just me and Muhammad in that small lobby. I tried to imagine what might be behind that curtain and why Muhammad was just sitting at a desk. He didn't look at me; he was singularly focused on doing absolutely nothing, and I guessed looking at me or talking to me would constitute doing something.

When Yusuf emerged from the alcove of secrets, he started asking questions. "What masjid do you go to?"

I stretched my brain even further. *Masjid. Masjid?*

Yusuf was speaking English, but the word *masjid* was Arabic. I took a sip of the scalding, sickeningly sweet tea to give myself a moment to think. I forced myself to ignore the pain on my tongue.

Masjid?

Mosque!

"What mosque do I go to?"

Why does he think I go to a mosque? Why did he call it a masjid if we're speaking English?

"I don't go to a mosque. I'm Catholic."

Yusuf sat down beside me. He slowly sipped his tea and smoothed out his thobe at the knees. He might have been the same age as me, but he carried himself like a philosophy professor or a high school principal.

I took an extra sip of the tea.

In a moment that felt like hours, I could see that Yusuf was looking at me as if I were a lost soul. And even though I was lost, I didn't feel lost. I felt alone. I felt afraid. But I did not feel lost. I felt like I was on the verge of living out the dream that had been born in me when 9/11 happened.

As I tried to look calm while burning my tongue and spiking my blood sugar, he asked me, "So, what brings you to the Ma'had?"

I knew *ma'had* didn't mean Egypt or the Middle East, so it must have something to do with the Institute where we were sitting. *Ma'had* must mean "institute." I projected confidence and just started talking.

"Well, I've been studying Arabic for a few months, but it felt like I wasn't learning as quickly as I wanted to. It is very important for me, well, for all Americans, to get a better idea of the Arabic language and Arab culture so we can have better relations. I know that there are a lot of things that we don't understand about Arab culture, and there may be some things that Arabs don't understand about American culture."

Yusuf remained silent, watching me carefully, so I blundered on nervously.

"I just started a graduate program in Islamic studies and want to make sure that I get a really good foundation in Arabic so I can understand the Qur'an and Islam. I know most of my friends don't know anything about the Middle East, and if I can learn as much as possible, then I can change the way average Americans think about these things."

I took a deep breath and sucked up another sip of tea. All those words just poured out of my mouth. I didn't know if Yusuf wanted to hear all that, but I had blurted it out before he had a chance to object. I must have been attention-deprived after a long couple of days of traveling because I rarely talked like that with anyone.

Yusuf remained calm and detached, asking, "What do you think about Islam?"

As Yusuf sipped away at his tea, I went from feeling like I was meeting someone to feeling like I was being interrogated. Part of me worried that I was digging myself into a hole that was going to end with me in a duffel bag in the back of a pickup truck on my way to Baghdad.

Another part of me kept talking. "Honestly, not very much. I have taken a couple of classes on the history of Islam, but not much else."

Yusuf never broke character. "Great, then you can come to the masjid with us."

I half expected him to hop up and drag me to the mosque on the spot, but he just sat there, slurped down the rest of his tea, stood up suddenly, and disappeared behind the curtain. He came back after a few seconds, asked if I was finished with my tea, and disappeared behind the curtain with my cup. Moments later he reemerged to say that Abu Ali was busy for the rest of the day and would not be able to greet me.

I just sat there for a moment while Yusuf talked to Muhammad.

Was Abu Ali behind the curtain? Had I failed my test? Had they called al-Qaeda?

I went into panic mode again.

Why had the conversation ended so abruptly? Why did I have to go to the mosque with them?

After some discussion with Muhammad, Yusuf turned to me and said that they had agreed on five hours of lessons per day. The work week in Egypt was six days, so I would have classes from Saturday to Thursday. The lessons in Arabic and Islamic theology would be broken up into a three-hour session in the morning and a two-hour session after lunch. Abu Ali had chosen Muhsin to be my instructor because he had just earned his PhD in Islamic theology from al-Azhar University and was an excellent teacher. Rent was $50 per month, and I should expect roommates in a few weeks.

With that, Yusuf announced he was busy for the rest of the day, quickly turned around, and exited the Institute.

And so began my new life—alone in Egypt. I still had no idea where I was. I sat down in that chair in the lobby for what seemed like an eternity. I knew I could probably get Muhammad to take me home since he wasn't doing anything, but I didn't want his help. I also didn't want to walk home by myself. I knew it would be the first right on the main road and then straight down the long street to my apartment building and then up two flights of stairs to the apartment directly across from the stairwell. But what then? I still hadn't eaten. I still hadn't called home.

I needed to get up, and if I was too stubborn to ask Muhammad for help, then I needed to figure it out on my own. I stood up and waved to Muhammad. After a moment of hesitation, he waved back, and I turned to walk out.

***

I took my time walking home and I started noticing things I missed when Muhammad was leading me. At the intersection of the main road and my street was a woman with a cart selling sodas, chips, and other snacks. Just as I was thinking about buying a soda, it dawned on me: *I don't have Egyptian money. I don't even know what Egyptian money is called.*

I turned around immediately and retraced my steps to the Institute. When I walked in, Muhammad looked up at me with faint recognition, and I uttered the phrase I had been practicing since I turned around.

"Maa 'indee fuluuuus." (I don't have any money.)

Muhammad laughed and my heart sank. My mind scrambled to figure out what I had done wrong. I knew all of those words from Arabic class and I knew they were in the correct order. Then it dawned on me that he was laughing because I had barely gotten two feet inside the building when I announced my poverty. At least I finally got a reaction out of him.

He mumbled some words and reached into his drawer and pulled out a small metal box. Inside the small metal box was plenty of Egyptian money. I had no idea what the exchange rate was so I gave Muhammad 100 American dollars and he gave me a wad of Egyptian money. I divvied the money up between my pants and my shirt to deceive potential robbers who, I guessed, wouldn't be smart enough to check all of my pockets. On my walk home, I decided that the easiest place to eat would be a shop I had passed by that served food in a plastic tub that came in three different sizes. The shop had a word scrawled across it that I couldn't translate.

Was it "Kishireee" or "Kasharee" or "Kushuree"? Whatever it was, it looked like a lot of food.

I saw a man walk up and nod toward the large tub, smack a coin down on the counter, and stand there while the guy dished up a bunch of food into the tub. It looked like exactly what I needed: a lot of food with minimal conversation. I hovered outside long enough to see a few people go through the same process, but not so long that I drew attention to myself.

I screwed up my courage and walked through the door.

"Salaam alaykum."

The man greeted me first, and I mumbled back, "Salaam alaykum."

He spoke more words to me, and I waited until I thought he was finished with the pleasantries and asking me what I wanted. I had to pay attention to his hand motions and where he was looking to make sure I pointed to the big tub at the right time. I pulled the fold of money out of my pocket and peeled off a bill with a five on it. He took it and gave me a handful of change.

I wanted to scream and shout and jump up and down. I wanted to raise my arms above my head and beat my chest. Maybe reading al-Qahira at the Cairo airport wasn't a big deal, but this was actually a big deal—I wasn't going to starve to death.

My meal was delicious, with two different kinds of pasta layered between some sort of sauce, lentils, and fried onions. Two small glass bottles on the table held a spicy red sauce and a garlicky green sauce. I dumped both of them in the tub and slurped down my meal forkful after plastic forkful. As I sat there scooping the last bit of lentils and red-green sauce into my mouth, I looked up, half embarrassed that someone might be watching me eat like a savage.

It was all starting to come together somehow. The more I was able to function, the more I started to feel like I could figure out Egypt. Reenergized, I started squinting at squiggles on street signs, passing cars, and other shops on the street. I began to psych myself up to actually speak some real Arabic. I didn't know it then, but kushuri is the Egyptian national dish, and there were shops making and selling it on almost every street corner in Cairo. I was participating in an Egyptian ritual of shoveling down pasta and beans as millions of people did every day.

With a feeling of triumph, I walked into the Internet café across the street. It was a long, narrow space with five computers along each side. Arabic lettering stretched across the left wall, made of white plaster. On the other side there were CD covers and pictures of famous American rappers like 50 Cent. I walked down the narrow path between the rows of computers, only two of which were occupied, to approach the guy behind the desk. He sat, his body twisted on the chair so he could lean to the side to read the computer screen in front of him rather than trying to bend over his belly.

I uttered what I hoped was the ubiquitous phrase: "Salaam alaykum."

"Wa alaykum a-salaam."

Thankfully, he wasn't looking for a conversation; he just handed me a slip of paper and pointed to a computer without uttering a word. I looked over my right shoulder to see where he was pointing and walked slowly toward computer number three. As I sat down, I could hear him speaking loudly and brushing his hands in the direction of computer number four. I dutifully slid over one spot, hoping I could make sense out of this interaction without having to speak Egyptian Arabic. To my surprise, everything on the computer was in English. The Start window. The time. The label for Internet Explorer. I exhaled for the first time. I was in my element now.

***

The worst part of my first hours in Egypt was not being able to communicate my thoughts. I could utter short words and phrases, but I wanted to be able to talk to someone about my flight and laugh about all the stupid stuff that worried me. I wanted to be able to discuss Islam at length and learn the things I thought had been missing in my studies. But everything around me was foreign, and I could not express my emotions to anyone who would listen.

When I sat down at that computer, I was transported to a different world, my world. I opened window after window on Internet Explorer to get connected with the real world. I found an email from Tommy, a friend from Arabic class—he asked if my head had been chopped off yet and when I was going to be back drinking with him at the bar. My friend Nate from Boulder told me that the Middle East was stupid—that was the entire content of his email. Once I'd looked at the websites that were important to me and had scanned the headlines, I sat back and exhaled.

When I finally left the Internet café, the streets were bustling with people buying produce, smoking hookah, and kicking soccer balls. I stopped on the sidewalk and looked left and right to soak in the nightlife of my new community. There weren't many women dressed in all black, but all the women had some sort of covering. The few faces I could see looked East African—tall, slender, and gorgeous. I stood there for a moment, watching the women sway their way through the streets in small groups, giggling and whiling away their night. It felt like the first time in my life that I had really stopped to see the world around me. Life, in just a few hours, had changed so dramatically that I was forced to notice even the smallest things—from the road beneath my feet to the people who swirled around me living their everyday lives.

Arabic and Allah

Every morning after I walked into my classroom located just off the lobby at the Institute, my instructor, Muhsin, began our lesson by closing my textbook and having me recite the vocabulary list as far back as I could remember. On the fifth day, I had to start with the last word we learned on day four and recite every word back to the first day. When my memory failed, he would pick words at random from the past few weeks and shake his head at how bad my Arabic was.

It was infuriating.

Muhsin didn't speak English, so even when he was trying to be helpful, he would explain Arabic words with other Arabic words, which meant that he had added another word to my ever-growing list of vocabulary. Muhsin hadn't ever had an English-speaking student before, and rather than speaking slowly, he just rattled off words in Arabic as I feverishly tried to write them down—in Arabic.

The worst days were when he stood over my shoulder as I struggled to write down what he was saying and he interrupted himself to correct my writing or point out a stray line that could be mistaken for a vowel, which, I could only imagine, would insult the mother of the Prophet and justify my beheading. Good days with Muhsin energized me, and bad days energized me more. If I was able to re-member my vocabulary back six or seven days, I would race out of the Institute and lock myself in my room to add three or four more words without looking at the book. On bad days, when Muhsin was doing his best to give me a hard time, I would sit up all night cor-recting my errors—trudging up the long, narrow path of speaking, reading, and writing Arabic fluently.

My apartment became my self-styled monastery, where I retreated in my devotion to the study of Arabic and Islam. I was no longer go-ing in circles between Lesia's house, Swift Hall, and the bar. Or home, school, work, and the fire station. I was going in circles between my apartment, the Institute, the kushuri joint, and the Internet café. My routine was monotonous, but it was sacred.

***

The longer I subjected myself to Muhsin's well-intentioned harass-ment, the more I wanted to use my new language skills to figure out why Muslims had blown up the Twin Towers. I started eating lunch with other students in the Institute's kitchen, and I was surprised at how quickly they began talking to me. Eventually, the students who spoke English began inviting me out for tea or dinner for falafel and shwarma. They asked me about my life and whether I wanted to convert to Islam. I always told them I was happily Catholic, and at first, they were polite about my refusal to convert. The ones who spoke English were all recent converts to Islam from the United States and Europe.

All of them practiced the same unusual behaviors. They stooped down on one knee when they drank a glass of water, always spoke in hushed tones, and never shook my hand. A few times when I was sitting in the lobby waiting for Muhsin, I noticed that every time a woman walked in, she was always covered from head to toe, and every man in the room looked down at the floor as she walked by. When she passed in front of them, they looked to the left as if the sight of her would set them on fire.

These behaviors seemed like a way for them to let each other know that they were on the same team. The more I studied Islamic theology at the Institute, the more I realized that they were all fundamentalists who adhered to the strictest interpretation of Islam—they were Wahhabis. All of their habits were a way for them to tell each other that they were committed to the cause of forcing Islamic values on the modern world. This wasn't just some Institute; this was a fundamentalist madrassa where people were taught the same things that terrorists were taught. There weren't any classes on firing weapons or building bombs, but these guys were true believers.

That realization, while out having dinner with the other students, only fueled my passion. I hadn't run away to the American University in Cairo to be around other Westerners. I redoubled my efforts—I was exactly where I wanted to be. The adventurer in me wanted to play their game, so I devised an experiment: the next time a woman walked into the building, I looked down at the ground like everyone else. Nothing happened. No one handed me a plaque inviting me into their little group. I did that a few times to see how it would be received, but there was never any acknowledgment. I didn't really expect a reaction, but I wondered if they would notice that I was trying to respect their customs and start talking to me more about their beliefs.

So I tried the other side of the experimental coin. One day, it was just me and Muhammad in the lobby when a woman walked in, and I offered her the traditional greeting. She was halfway through introducing herself when she stopped suddenly and stared at me through the eye slit in her head covering. She was as shocked as I was hesitant. She made a movement toward me, slowed her gait, and caught herself mid-turn and redirected her energy toward Muhammad's desk. It probably shocked her that someone had spoken to her, and she temporarily forgot about the rules of engagement between men and women. I felt excited and nervous. At the same time, her reaction made me realize that I probably should have left her out of my experiment on fundamentalist Muslim behavior.

As I sat there in the metal chair trying to hide from Muhammad's glare, it was obvious that I had broken a rule that no one had told me about. It was an unspoken language that mattered as much as Arabic. No one said anything when I looked away from women in the lobby because it was the only language they knew. I was missing out on something important by not having friends at the Institute, and I needed to find a way to fix that problem.

**

Then, two people moved into my apartment. I went from roaming the empty rooms reciting vocabulary at all hours of the day to living with two American converts to Islam who instantly made friends with students at the Institute and turned my apartment into a social hub.

The first person to move in was Darius, a big African American guy in his late thirties. He'd left his wife and kids back in Philly so he could learn Arabic and become a prayer leader in his mosque. He was a hapless and funny man who obviously wanted people to like him. Back in Philly, he had a business selling trinkets at 30th Street Station. I instantly liked him because he seemed like the kind of guy who loved to have a good time. Most importantly, I thought he might be able to teach me why some fundamentalists wanted to kill Americans.

I learned Darius's life story within thirty minutes of him moving in. After spending the past year drinking at clubs, he had recently recommitted his life to Islam and started wearing a skullcap and thobe. A couple of weeks later, Michael, a college kid on summer break from Ohio State University, joined us. He studied chemical engineering and in his freshman year decided to convert to Islam like his parents. This was his first visit to the Middle East, and he was hoping to one day become an imām (religious leader) wherever he settled down. He reminded me of most engineering students I knew: serious and quiet. During discussions in our living room, he listened to the conversation and only spoke when he was addressed directly. The arrival of roommates transformed my solitary routine—I was ready to put my new learning to use. Finally, I was going to befriend real, live Muslims who could explain why terrorists did what they did.

The first thing I learned was that the brothers at the Institute took Islamic teachings to the extremes. They believed they were creating a radical break from modern, materialistic, heathen culture and instituting true Islamic values. One day, I was relaxing after class in our apartment with Darius, Michael, and another American who taught English at the Institute, Gabriel, a creature all to himself. Like most people at the Institute, he had come to Egypt after converting to Islam, but by the time we met, he had been in Egypt for four years and had already been married and divorced and had run out of money. He overstayed his tourist visa and was working at the Institute to save up money to get back home. Although he carried something of a jokester disposition, it was obvious that being stuck in a foreign country with no way home was an awful life.

I had grown used to listening to them talk about the Qur'an, why they had converted, and what they hoped to accomplish during their time in Egypt. They talked about Muslims in America and the difficulties of remaining true to their faith amid the temptations of mainstream American life. Michael talked about wanting to find an American Muslim girl who would be willing to wear traditional garb, and Darius worried about his kids getting hooked on drugs. Gabriel always wanted to talk about the state of the world and how Muslims needed to rise up against the infidels.

In the middle of the conversation, Gabriel made a statement that shocked me: "Hitler had it right with the Jews. They have never been anything but trouble for all of history, and we would all be better off if they were just exterminated."

He kept talking, and I was so enraged that I didn't hear him. But I was also curious. I wondered how Darius and Michael would react.

Every one of us was surprised by what Gabriel had said. Michael just put his head down and disengaged from the conversation. Darius looked around the room like a kid trying to steal a piece of Thanksgiving turkey from the kitchen counter; glancing briefly at each of us to see how he should act. I could tell he was trying to figure out how the person he wanted to be should respond to that situation.

When I realized that Darius would not say anything, I finally spoke up.

"That's completely unacceptable!"

I went on a rant. I rejected Gabriel's words and demanded he take them back. Darius looked at me and then at Gabriel and Michael. And then he chimed in.

"I don't know, maybe Gabriel has a point…"

It seemed that Darius didn't want to defend Gabriel, but his recent recommitment to Islam made it difficult for him to know how he should react. Gabriel was the worst kind of bully. He had an audience of new converts who were lost in Egypt and didn't know any better. He thought his status as a teacher at the Institute afforded him the right to wield the kind of authority that shouldn't be questioned. He didn't force Darius to agree with him by pointing a gun at his head, but there was an unspoken threat of excommunication. Darius felt he had to prove he was committed to the strict interpretations of the Qur'an accepted by everyone else at the Institute. I was angry with Gabriel, but I felt sorry for Darius and Michael.

When anger overran my curiosity, I stormed out of the room and refused to talk to any of them for weeks. I ate meals in my room and only spent time in the apartment when I was sleeping or studying. I couldn't believe that Americans, Muslims or not, would buy into the things that Gabriel had said.

I avoided them assiduously until Darius pulled me aside one day on the main road outside the Institute and made his confession: "I should never have agreed with him. What he said about Hitler was wrong, and I know it."

"I understand, man," I said. "Don't worry about it."

"Islam doesn't support that kind of language or behavior, and I hope you'll forgive me and not think badly about Islam."

"I forgive you," I said, even though I didn't.

I couldn't forgive him because he wasn't apologizing for the right thing: violating his own conscience. I wasn't worried that he would go back to the United States and start a genocide against Jews; I was worried that he would go back to the United States and start doing and saying whatever the other crazy fundamentalists had told him to do. It scared me that people like him, people who seemed like me in a lot of ways, could wind up doing horrible things because they wanted to fit in.

Word of my outburst quickly spread throughout the brothers studying at the Institute, and eventually Abu Ali, the owner of the Institute, sat me down for a talk.

"The brothers are concerned about you, Alexander."

Try as I might, I couldn't get anyone to recognize that my name was not a shortened form of Alexander.

"What are they worried about?"

"They are concerned that you are going to use what you are learning here to attack Islam in your research."

I noticed that Abu Ali used *concerned* instead of *worried*, and I didn't think it was because English was his second language.

"Abu Ali, I really want to learn about Islam. I don't want to hurt you or your religion. I am studying because I believe there is a way for the Muslim and Western world to get along. To understand each other better. I hope you believe me."

Abu Ali said he believed me, but I knew he was lying. My refusal to convert was the only thing they cared about.

Abu Ali was a stately figure. He rarely showed up at the Institute, but his reputation was that of a cultural giant. When he took a second wife, he didn't go out and find the youngest available woman; he went out and found an older, unattractive widow who had two young boys living at home. When he married her, he followed Islamic law exactly: he bought an apartment for his new wife that was no worse but no better than that of his first wife. Islamic law required that the second through fourth wives were treated exactly the same as the first wife in terms of time, money, and affection spent. Abu Ali's decision made him something of a rock star among the brothers at the Institute, who tried to find any way they could to impose a medieval mindset onto the modern world.

***

Cairo changed me in a way that was familiar. I still loved Saint Francis, hated Barry, and regularly emailed my dad, even though he had no idea why I was obsessed with the Middle East. My passion to fix US–Middle Eastern relations started off like every other mission: I was mesmerized by some event that I couldn't quite explain and immersed myself in an entirely new kind of life to make sense out of the incomprehensible. But the Middle East was a drug I couldn't live without. If it didn't have to do with me being in the Middle East or preparing to be in the Middle East, I didn't care about it. I lost track of Bret for years, I didn't talk to Father James again until I was back in D.C., and I never made it back to the Lionville Fire Department. All of the things—the relationships—that used to define me were cast aside.

Abed

One of the first conversations I had with Marvin Wilde when I returned to Chicago reinforced the need for me to keep pursuing my dream.

"Did you get what you wanted out of Egypt?" he asked.

"Somewhat. I can speak Arabic, and I read a lot from the Qur'an and Islamic law, but I still don't feel like I understand fundamentalist Muslims."

"Well," he said, leaning in, "if you want to understand this movement, you need to understand the people and what they care about."

I didn't know any fundamentalists in Chicago, so memorizing the Qur'an became my newest obsession. I replaced all of the music on my iPod with a recitation by Sa'ad al-Ghamdi because I knew the Qur'an was the most important text for Muslims. Sa'ad was a Saudi tenor whose voice was so clear and powerful that it could tell the story of the Qur'an for people who didn't understand Arabic. The Qur'an is vivid in its descriptions, but when Sa'ad recited it, I could see myself soaring through the sky or sitting at the feet of the angel

Gabriel. His voice reminded me of Gregorian chant and transported me to another world where I began to understand the power of the Qur'an. I devoted myself to the Qur'an in a way that felt deeply personal, and it helped me understand the spiritual life of Islam.

Memorizing the Qu'ran is an exact science, and I scoured books in Arabic and English to learn every rule. There were places where you had to pause and other places where you could not pause. Certain sounds had to be omitted in specific situations, and there were a few passages that required you to prostrate as you recited a verse. It wasn't good enough to just memorize the words. I needed to know other things, such as when to elongate certain vowels or lower the volume of my voice.

I hoped that memorizing the Qur'an would help me interact with Muslims better, but the more I memorized, the more it changed my perspective on Islam. It taught me about Islam, and reciting the Qur'an became my own spiritual exercise. I started to feel the awe that Muslims talk about when they describe their commitment to the message of Allah. It wasn't just the words or the history that I was learning; it was the passion in Sa'ad's voice. He lamented the disobedience of sinners with such conviction that it changed the way I thought about Islam's call to religious obedience. By the winter of 2004, I was obsessed with the Qur'an and carried a copy everywhere I went. I blocked out the world rushing past the train window by dragging my finger across the page to the rhythm of Sa'ad's powerful voice. Once again, I created my own monastic cell in the midst of a chaotic life that couldn't fulfill my deep passion to change the world.

***

One day, I was sitting in Pick Hall where I had my Arabic classes, reviewing a difficult passage in Chapter Five of the Qur'an, when one of the students who was Muslim asked me what I was doing.

"I'm reading Sura al-Māʾida. I'm trying to memorize it, but it's kicking my ass."

He walked away with a confused look on his face.

A few days later, one of the graduate teaching assistants, Abed, stopped me in the hallway and asked why I was memorizing the Qur'an. "Oh," I said, and paused for a moment. "How did you know I was memorizing the Qur'an?" I had talked to Abed only a few times.

"I just heard someone talking about it the other day."

I wasn't sure if Abed was a friend, so I redirected the conversation. "When I was in Cairo, I saw a five-year-old recite the entire Qur'an by heart, so I figured if he can do it, then I can, too."

I chuckled, but Abed continued, "Did you watch the whole thing?"

"No, but everyone told me he had been at it for hours. Why? Did you memorize the Qur'an?"

"How much have you memorized?"

The questioning seemed to be turning into an interrogation, but I decided to see where things were going. "I've memorized the last section and the first half of the first section." I was proud that I could recite the Qur'an for 45 minutes without having to look at the words on a page.

"Yeah, right."

"I did." I laughed a little to break the ice and repeated my previous sentence in Arabic so he knew I meant business: "hafathtu juz' al-thālith wa nusf al-ūla."

"Wow. Good job."

I couldn't tell whether he was being sarcastic.

"Am I smarter than a five-year-old?"

Abed finally broke into a smile. "There are some people who don't like that you are memorizing the Qur'an."

"What? Why?"

"Who cares? Did you eat dinner yet?"

Abed put his arm around my shoulder, and as we walked to the restaurant Medici on 57th, we became best friends. We started spending all of our free time together—I was looking for a teacher, and he was looking for a student. He helped me memorize the Qur'an by quizzing me on specific sections and also started teaching me hadīth, religious stories about the Prophet Muhammad. Abed explained that the Qur'an was the most important book in Islam but that it did not answer all the questions people have about their faith. Fundamentalists rely more on hadīth to justify their beliefs than the Qur'an. Abed wasn't just teaching me the words on the page; he was explaining why fundamentalists thought the way they did.

Abed was Egyptian, but he grew up outside Houston eating barbecue, dating cheerleaders, and doing the things high school boys do. His parents never went to the mosque, and he had never known what it meant to be a Muslim until he got his heart broken in college. Just like the brothers at the Institute, Abed was a convert. We were sitting in Regenstein Library when he told me his story.

"I fell in love with a girl in high school right before she left for college in Canada. She wanted to get as far away from Houston as possible, and I couldn't imagine my life without her. When she told me I should follow my own dreams, I told her she was the only dream worth having…

"…then I found her with another guy, and I wanted to end my life.

"I started going to the mosque because I didn't know what else to do. *Islam* means 'submission' in Arabic, and I didn't have any family or friends to turn to—God was my only choice. I don't know what would have happened if I hadn't embraced Islam completely."

"I know what you mean. I found Jesus at a low point in my life as well."

"Do you actually go to church?"

"Yes, I actually go to church. I usually go a few times a week; there's a good priest on campus."

"That's good. Most Christians I know don't go to church. They don't really believe in God."

Abed was a convert who had become a fundamentalist, but I quickly learned he was very different from the brothers at the Institute. He believed that the Taliban and al-Qaeda weren't real Muslims because they violated one of the most important rules in Islam: Muslims must obey their political leaders. He taught me that Islam didn't separate religion and politics and that there were certain political rules that were as important as religious duties.

"Al-Qaeda is shit. They are like the apostates from early Islam who killed people who didn't agree with them. They killed *Muslims*! They are shit. The Taliban pick from the Qur'an or Ḥadīth, whatever aligns with their shit brains, even though all the religious scholars agree that you can't kill Muslims."

"Then why do so many people follow them?"

"Because people are stupid. They don't understand their religion and they follow whatever shit they hear. If people studied the true religion, they would never be tricked by them."

I had never heard anyone talk like Abed before. He didn't try to explain away the violence in the Qur'an like most of the professors and students I studied with. Abed was a fundamentalist who was proud of his religion. He didn't have any problem with chopping people's heads off or stoning women, but he knew that those acts had to happen under certain conditions. Al-Qaeda and the Taliban, he always told me, were corrupt, power-hungry thugs who knew and cared nothing about the truth of fundamentalist Muslim rules. It was a subject we talked about over and over.

"The purpose of true religion, real Islam, is to bring peace to the world, not terrorize it. The Qur'an is only harsh on people who would disrupt the natural order of the world."

"But don't you think Muslims need to update their teachings? Christians used to have all sorts of stupid rules, but we figured out how to modernize."

"Alexs."

He never called me Alexander.

"You need to understand something. Just because Christians and Muslims have a lot in common, don't forget this: the Qur'an is the literal word of Allah. We don't get to pick and choose from the Qur'an; we just follow it."

"But…"

"There is no *but*!"

Abed was yelling. "If you apply your logic to Islam, especially fundamentalists, you will never understand what's going on. These people aren't playing a game. They aren't killing themselves because they're crazy or poor; they are trying to live up to the Word of Allah. You can't solve terrorism until you understand how they think about their religion, not how you think they should think about their religion."

"Listen, people join violent religious movements because they're poor or afraid," I yelled back at him, "and that's true of violent Muslim groups, too."

The more times he yelled at me about Islam, the more I realized that the theories I was learning in the Divinity School felt hollow. I didn't agree with chopping people's heads off, but there was something about the way Abed talked about religion that my studies couldn't explain. At about the same time, Abed and I both realized that I needed to study Islam from the inside out. One day, toward the end of the school year, we were on one of our daily walks through Hyde Park when he told me that he was going back to Alexandria, Egypt.

"You mean for the summer?"

He put his arm around my shoulder.

"I'm not sure if I'm coming back. The mosque I go to found me a wife, and we are getting married next week. My adviser treats me like shit and calls me a crazy fundamentalist. For all I know, she won't accept my dissertation even after I've put all these years into it. I'm just sick of the shit here, and ever since my parents retired to Egypt, my mom keeps asking when I'm coming home."

"So you're not coming back? What the hell am I supposed to do, big brother?"

"You should come to Alex with me."

"Alexandria?"

"Yeah, we can study together at my home. You won't be distracted with the shit going on here."

"You mean for the summer?"

"You can stay as long as you want."

I didn't hesitate. "Okay, I'll go."

Abed was an American who knew how to explain the urgency fundamentalists felt about instituting a new world order. He yelled at me when I reduced it all to ignorance and challenged me to put myself in the mindset of someone who was willing to die for God's will. Most importantly, he fueled my passion. Somehow, he understood that I was a bottomless fountain of obsessive energy that needed a mission to feel complete. Rather than encouraging me to live a normal graduate school life, Abed pushed me to be more committed, even more focused, and ruthlessly devoted to the mission. It felt like Abed understood me in a way that no one ever had, and he became my most important relationship for nearly five years.

***

When I graduated with my master's degree in divinity and prepared to start my PhD coursework, there was no hesitation—I hopped on another airplane to Cairo. This time, I made my own way to Tahrir Square and found a bus north to Alex. When I got off the bus, Abed was nowhere to be found, and the phone number he gave me just rang and rang until I hung up in frustration. I wandered around the bus station for a few minutes before someone told me that there was a trolley to downtown Alexandria. Abed had never told me where he lived in Alexandria, but I figured downtown would be close enough to wherever we decided to meet.

The moment the trolley took off, I knew Alex was different than Cairo. Public transportation in Cairo was always packed, with bodies smashed against bodies that were poised to dash through barely opened doors. The Alexandria trolley was clean, with nice wooden benches and a conductor who politely asked for tickets. No one argued with him or tried to negotiate for a cheaper fare, and there were no deviations from the planned schedule. Cairo was a dusty urban jungle, but the scenery in Alexandria was breathtaking. From the right side of the trolley I could see the sun setting over the Mediterranean Sea, and on the left I could see parents hauling groceries and children into apartment complexes. Near the end of the line, the train crested a hill that gave me a bird's-eye view of downtown Alexandria. The massive Sofitel hotel emerged against a backdrop of crowds meandering along the Corniche—the main road that hugged the coastline. I could hear the water crashing against the shores, and there were palm trees swaying in the wind in front of the big sign on top of the building that spelled out S-O-F-I-T-E-L in English letters. If I could have replaced the Arabic being spoken around me with French or Italian, I would have thought I was in Europe.

When the train stopped at its final destination, I tried calling Abed again, but there was still no answer. While I tried to figure out what to do, I stopped at a restaurant near the train station and ordered my favorite meal, kushuri. After lingering at the restaurant until my presence there became uncomfortable, I tried Abed one more time. There was still no answer, so I asked the doorman at the restaurant if he knew any hotels in the area. It was as if he hadn't heard my question; he just launched into the first thought that came across his mind.

"Min wayn, anta?" (Where are you from?)

The doorman was trying to size me up. We were speaking Arabic, but he could tell that it wasn't my native language.

"Ana Amrīkī." (I'm American.)

"Aywah habībī, fī fundūq hunāk, al-Sofitel." (Of course, my friend, the Sofitel is right there.)

"La'a habībī, b-ayaz fundūq 'aamī." (No, my friend, I want a hotel for locals.)

I was living on a student's budget and didn't have the money to stay at an expensive Western-style hotel, so I needed something that charged Egyptian rates—closer to $20 a day. No matter how much I pressed, though, the doorman didn't want to give me any other options; he just couldn't believe that an American would want to stay in a hotel for Egyptians. Finally, after we reached the point of almost yelling at each other, he pointed me in the direction of a nice little Egyptian hotel above the only liquor store in Alexandria.

The young man behind the desk told me that a room would cost 35 guinay (Egyptian pounds), or $7 per day, and it came with a continental breakfast but had a shared bathroom. I asked to see the room, and it had a large bed, a desk with a chair, and a large window that looked down onto the building's courtyard. Everything was clean enough and cheap enough, so I reserved it for one month.

It wasn't until later the next day, after I'd gotten settled in my new environment, that I got hold of Abed, and we agreed to meet the following morning. At the bus station, I ran up and gave him a hug.

"Where were you? I missed you, a<u>kh</u>ī." (Brother.)

I could tell from the way he looked at me that he was embarrassed.

"I'm sorry, little brother. I had a migraine attack, and I've been in bed for the past few days."

I put my arm around his shoulder. "I'm sorry. Are you feeling better?"

"I'm fine, but enough about that. What section of the Qur'an are you memorizing?"

He wrapped my arm in his, and we began our first lesson. Abed pushed me unceasingly. When I arrived at his house at 8:00 a.m. the next morning to start my training, he yelled at me for being late. When I started dozing off at 10:00 p.m., he banged on the table and told me I wasn't committed enough. I showed up at 7:00 a.m the next day. Then 6:00 a.m. I buried my nose in dusty old theology textbooks and scribbled notes until well after midnight because that's what was expected of me. I believed that Abed was the only person

I knew who could help me accomplish my mission. That's how I spent my summer and most of the next fall quarter, walking the Mediterranean, hand in hand with Abed, getting yelled at every time I mispronounced a word or couldn't recite a line of text from memory from the books we'd read weeks prior.

We were best friends. Abed loved me, and I loved him more. Every week, I brought his wife groceries for the house—I never knew where all the food went since I also bought him three meals a day. Everything was cheaper in Alex. I didn't just pay for his meals; I ordered for him, picked up his meals from the counter at the restaurant, and prepared his tea. For breakfast, he liked fūl—smashed fava beans—with scrambled eggs and tea; fast food for lunch; and seafood for dinner. Wherever Abed went, I followed. Every situation was an opportunity for me to learn more about Islam or Egypt. If we were waiting in line to pay, he would quiz me on numbers or the names of different fruit. If we were at a restaurant, he would have me explain the religious laws for ritual purity. He'd be playing with his nieces and nephews, and I'd be stuck in a corner trying to parse some passage about the distinction between free will and predestination. We usually spent more than twelve hours a day with each other before I walked him to his house and rushed back to a bar on the Corniche to banter with the Coptic Christians. By the end of our time together, when Abed asked me difficult questions, I could effortlessly cite the Qur'an and medieval theologians—I started to think like a fundamentalist.

We created our own version of a French salon with a flavor of medieval tutelage. Abed was my patron and I was his muse. He was rich beyond my wildest dreams when it came to the one thing I cared about: fixing relations between the United States and Middle Eastern countries. For every question I asked him, he could recite verses from the Qur'an or ḥadīth or some obscure text. I didn't know it at the time, but when Abed and I first met, he had been unhappy with graduate school, single, and lonely. I became his excuse to be singularly focused on his faith. We helped each other.

The Fundamentalist Within

When I got back to Chicago, I hit the streets of Hyde Park with a vengeance. I was proud of my crash course in fundamentalist thinking, but I relieved the pressures by drinking as much as possible. I was just getting ready to get back into my coursework in the fall when I got a phone call from a number I didn't recognize.

"Is this Alexs?"

"Yes, who is this?"

"This is Professor Marshall. I have a unique opportunity, and when it came across my desk, I immediately thought of you."

"Okay, what is it?"

"I spoke at the National Seminary in Muscat, Oman, last year, and the dean of the school has asked me if I have any students who would want to do a study abroad there this year."

I didn't stop to think or ask any questions. "I'll go."

"Great, can you come by my office next week?"

"I will. See you next week."

Professor Dennis Marshall was one of the most important scholars in Islamic history in the world, and I was shocked that he had thought of me. It would be a chance for me to learn about a completely different culture in the Middle East and devote myself to the full-time study of Islamic theology again.

I called my buddy Tommy right away and told him, "I'm going back to the Middle East in a few weeks."

"In a few weeks?"

"Yeah, Professor Marshall got me into the National Seminary in Oman."

"Didn't you just sign a lease on a new place for the school year?"

"Oh, yeah…"

"Didn't you just get back from Alexandria?"

"Yeah…"

When we met up for dinner at Salonica, Tommy was still peppering me with questions that I didn't know how to answer.

"Are you sure you want to take off for another year? Are you going to be ready for qualifying exams?"

"I don't know, Tommy, but this is a once-in-a-lifetime opportunity. Have you ever met anyone who studied there? Hell, have you ever met someone who's been to Oman?"

"No."

I felt like I had to justify my decision. "The Omanis practice a different kind of Islam that very few people know about, and I can be one of the few people who understands it. Some people say modern Islamic terrorism originates in their sect."

"I already know all that. What the fuck are you doing with your life, dude?"

The predominant sect of Islam in Oman was called Ibādism, which was only practiced in Oman and parts of Libya. The Ibādis were descendants of the Kharijites, who were the first Muslims to call for the assassination of other Muslims. The Kharijites terrorized Iraq in the seventh century, demanding that other Muslims accept their theology or be killed. The Ibādis, who settled in Oman and Libya, weren't a violent group, but they preserved a lot of the theology of the Kharijites. I had a theory that the Ibādis would be the perfect group to study how violent Muslims transitioned into nonviolence and hoped to apply that theory to modern terrorists.

Two weeks later, I was on an airplane to another foreign country in the Middle East, fueled by a belief that I could single-handedly solve all the problems in US–Middle Eastern relations. When I landed at Seeb International Airport in Muscat, Oman, I was fluent enough in Modern Standard and Egyptian Arabic that I didn't have any trouble making my way through immigration and out to the arrivals pickup lane, where I met the driver who would take me to my new adventure.

It was the middle of the night when we finally pulled up to the four-story stone building that would be my home for the next year. The driver helped me throw my bags into an empty room on the first floor that had four beds with four desks and chairs. I drifted off to sleep.

The next morning, David, one of the seminary students, woke me up around 7:00 a.m. to go shopping. Apparently, he had heard that I would be arriving and had taken it upon himself to help me get situated during the first few days. He took me on a quick tour of the first floor of the dorm and then across the street to a few clothing stores. David was from a rural town outside of Accra, Ghana, and he explained one of the benefits of studying in Oman.

"Everyone at the Seminary gets a check from the government of Oman every month, and it's much more money than I would make back in Ghana, so I get a good education and I am able to send money home to my family."

David spoke English well enough for us to understand one another, but we spoke in Arabic so I could practice. He did his best to help me fit in. By the late morning, we were standing in one of the local shops in the Ruwi neighborhood of Muscat, trying on a dishdasha and a kumma. The dishdasha is the dress worn by Muslims all over the world, and the kumma is a small white cylindrical hat embroidered with colors like brown or dark blue.

As David pushed the dishdasha into my hands, I couldn't even imagine how ridiculous I would look.

"I don't think it's a good idea for me to dress like an Omani since I'm not a Muslim."

"Trust me, it will be easier if you wear the traditional dress. You will blend in more."

"Don't you think people will be offended that I'm imitating their religion?"

"I think you'll stick out if you walk around in American clothes."

I didn't know David at all, but I could tell after a few hours that his only intention was to help me. He wasn't trying to impose his viewpoints on me; he was just being kind. So I walked out of that shop with my khaki pants and button-down shirt in a bag, wearing an Omani-style dishdasha and kumma. The transformation was swift but complete: not only did I know how to think like a fundamentalist, but I also looked like one.

Oman was a much more traditional country than Egypt. In Egypt, everyone wore whatever they want, especially in the major cities. Women wore as little or as much clothing as they pleased in Cairo, but in Muscat, women were always completely covered. Omanis were a mixture of Arab, Indian, and African, and almost anyone who wore Omani dress looked Omani. David and I were speaking in Arabic and both of us were wearing dishdashas—I completely blended in.

Once we dropped off my old clothes, David showed me to the cafeteria, helped me get my meal, and taught me how to eat with my hands. The meals were served on small metal elementary school platters and usually included half of a chicken, three piles of rice, and some sort of vegetable but no utensils. We all sat on the floor in a large room using our hands to pick off pieces of chicken and fold it in a ball of rice before stuffing it into our mouths.

Most of the students around me laughed as rice and bits of chicken dribbled from my mouth to the floor.

David joined in on the laughter. "Even a child knows how to eat!"

I didn't know how to respond to the laughter, so I kept spreading grains of rice around with my hands until I came up with a system to get food in my mouth. It was humiliating but exhilarating. In just a few hours, I could see that Oman was completely different than Egypt and that I was going to have experiences I could never have anticipated. In Oman, I wasn't a PhD student; I didn't even know how to feed myself. I was unexpectedly excited; my knowledge of fundamentalism would be stretched even further than what I had learned in my studies in Cairo and Alexandria. I wasn't just standing on the outside watching Muslims; I was wearing what they wore, living with them, and—eventually—eating the way they ate.

David and I spent the rest of the day walking around Ruwi and talking about what it was like at the Seminary. When night fell, he dropped me off in my empty room and disappeared up the stairs. I fell asleep on my second night in Oman, dreaming about how much I would learn over the next school year.

The dean of the National Seminary and Professor Marshall had decided to put me through the freshman course curriculum. When I woke up the next morning, I began my classes in Qur'anic studies, hadīth, Arabic grammar, and other religious courses. All of my classes were taught in Arabic, just me and forty eighteen-year-old Bedouin farmers who had never met a non-Muslim, a non-Arabic speaker, or an American. It was like being an alien in a one-room schoolhouse. I struggled to understand our instructors, whose accents spanned the Arab world. Between the textbooks and the lectures, I managed to pick up about 85 percent of the materials we were studying. I went into my normal monastic routine of obsessing about my studies, spending every moment outside class reading and memorizing the lessons we had learned that day.

For the first few weeks, I didn't have any friends besides David. The students in my class treated me like the new kid: they threw crumpled paper at me when I wasn't looking and laughed at me when I mispronounced words. As I walked in the room, they made snide remarks I couldn't understand, and if we read about how to treat non-Muslims, they would slide their desks further away from me.

Thankfully, a few weeks later, I was studying in my room when a student came bounding in and sat down on my bed, asking in Arabic, "Is your name Alexander?"

"Yes, what's your name?"

"My name is Abdullah. I heard that you were studying here and I had to come meet you."

He stood up and shook my hand before sitting back down on the bed.

"How do you like it here?"

"Oh, it's great. I didn't know anything about Oman or Ibādism before I got here, and now I'm learning a lot."

"You don't know about our religion?"

"No, not really."

"Great, then I'll teach you religion, and you'll teach me English."

And that was that. We were best friends.

Abdullah was twenty with the energy of a twelve-year-old. He was curious about everything he saw and wanted to know where I was from and why I was at the Seminary.

"What is America like? I mean, where in America are you from? What's it like there?"

The questions were just tumbling out of his mouth, and I barely had time to answer one before he exploded with the next. I picked up on his energy and started firing off questions to him.

"Where in Oman are you from?"

"I'm from a village near Nizwa. Have you heard of Nizwa?"

"No, where is it?"

"Where is it?" Abdullah laughed. "Nizwa was once the most important city in Oman—our first capital and where the imāms lived…you really don't know?"

"No, I'm sorry. But you can teach me."

We went on like that for most of the night, talking about the things that mattered most to us. He didn't know exactly how, but he believed speaking better English and understanding American culture would help his future, and I knew that he could help me understand fundamentalist Islam better.

As Abdullah was walking out the door just after midnight, he turned and nervously asked me, "Would you like to come live with me in my room? There's an extra bed and desk, and no one sleeps there now."

"Yes, that would be awesome. When can I move in?"

Abdullah started grabbing my things and said, "Right now. Let's go, brother."

It didn't take long for me to realize that Abdullah was the brightest and most well-known student at the Seminary. When David learned that Abdullah had invited me to live with him, he congratulated me with a slap on the back. Abdullah was a third-year student, and he always scored the highest on all of the exams.

One day, we were both studying in our room and he could tell that I was struggling. "Are you okay?" he asked.

"No. I'm studying Omani history, but I just can't make sense of this one sentence."

I always spoke Arabic with him and he spoke English with me.

"Which book is it?"

I held up the textbook and he nodded.

"Which part don't you understand? Read it to me."

I started reading from the first line of the page, and after a few words he started reciting along with me without looking at the page. Once I realized what he was doing, I stopped in shock and looked at him as he continued reciting.

He asked, "Which part don't you understand?"

I looked quickly down at the passage.

"Uhhhh…it's two more lines. Wait? Did you memorize this whole book?"

Abdullah just laughed and tried to figure out where I was having trouble. "Do you mean the part where it is talking about the period of the Imāmate and the Sultanate?"

I was dumbfounded. He hadn't read that textbook in two years, but he still remembered it word for word. I thought he must have been playing a trick on me, so we made a game of it. I picked random pages from all of my textbooks and eventually the Qur'an as he effortlessly finished sentences and paragraphs before I had uttered a few words.

Abdullah was like the rest of the kids at the Seminary who had moved away from their families in the deserts of Oman. They were the brightest boys in their town and had been shipped off to the big city to learn to be religious leaders. All of them were suspicious of outsiders and definitely suspicious of non-Muslims. I hadn't known it, but the administration had spent weeks trying to find volunteers who were willing to live with a non-Muslim. For fundamentalists, the rules of Islam are clear: Muslims and non-Muslim should not be living together.

But in many ways, Abdullah was different. He was the smartest student and, I would learn, the most open-minded fundamentalist at the Seminary. He had a similar independent spirit of adventure that made us best friends. Because of his kindness and curiosity, we wound up spending all of our free time together. Abdullah's dream was to be an imām in Muscat, not in his hometown. He knew that he would have to go back home for a few years, but ultimately, he wanted to be a famous preacher who helped people understand their religion. He was a true believer and explained every aspect of why the Ibādis believed what they did and why his religion was better than mine. He was never mean or disrespectful, just honest.

Abdullah lectured me on how the Apostles had misunderstood Jesus's message and that the true message of Jesus was recorded in the Qur'an. He showed me how to eat soup with my fingers and pray with the Shi'ites. He took me to see his family home in the desert and explained the importance of the monuments and royal palaces in Oman. He taught me to fast Ramadān and took me to the community meals (iftār) after sunset. If I had learned how to think like a fundamentalist from Abed, I learned how to live like a fundamentalist from Abdullah.

Abdullah was the kind of fundamentalist who wasn't radicalized; he didn't believe that violence was the answer to the world's problems. He repeated the same lesson every other fundamentalist had told me: the word *Islam* means "submission." Abdullah believed that it was his job to invade the modern world with a medieval sensibility because modern people were too focused on their rights and had forgotten about their obligations to God. True peace, he taught me, was found in extinguishing one's will in pursuit of true submission to God. He believed that the terrorists were wrong because they didn't have the authority to carry out God's judgment, not because they interpreted Islamic law incorrectly.

I could tell that Abdullah was a true believer because of how he lived his life. When he told me that he loved me, it was pure and inspiring. He didn't use anger to convince himself that he was better than other people; his faith was effortless and inviting. I was starting to understand that there were two kinds of fundamentalist Muslims: those whose passion for God was motivated by love, and others who were motivated by anger. Abdullah's kind of fundamentalism reminded me of the monks in Virginia—they believed deeply that the world was out of sync with God's will, and they devoted all their energy to being a bright light in a darkened world. Terrorist fundamentalists weren't patient enough for that kind of life. Abdullah wanted change, but he started with himself and then gave freely to those around him.

I started to understand fundamentalists and terrorists in a completely different way. Since 9/11, the one thing that I understood about terrorists was their joyful acceptance of unthinkable destruction. Violence was the most important principle in their religion, psyche, culture, and history. Images of the Pentagon burning and firefighters blanched in ash crowded out any ability for me to understand the passion that motivated those people. Everyone explained violent Muslim fundamentalists with the word *terror*, but I was coming to realize that the violence was blinding us to a deeper reality that Abed had tried to explain to me. Terrorists weren't obsessed with violence; they were obsessed with bringing peace to the everyday world.

When I studied in Egypt, I had always been able to turn my studies on when I was in class and put them aside when I was out drinking at the bar. It was in Oman that I stopped being able to turn it on and off. Thinking like a fundamentalist became a part of who I was.

Yemen

"They kidnap Americans in Yemen. For fun. Don't go!"

Abdullah was trying to talk me out of my latest hare-brained idea, but I wouldn't back down.

"Abdullah, I'll probably never be in this part of the world again. I need to understand the Middle East as much as possible, so I'm going to Yemen."

"Yemen!? They're all backward and dirty. Just stay here with me, and I'll teach you everything you need to know about them."

"Thanks, a<u>kh</u>ī, but I already bought my tickets. You should come with me."

"No way. No chance. I've never been and I'll never go. They are savages down there."

"But if I get kidnapped, you can talk us out of it."

"Are you serious? They'll kidnap us and then kill me for the fun of it. They ransom Americans; they kill Arabs."

"Oh…"

"Yeah. They don't care about Arabs. They just want Americans for their money."

"Really?"

"Yeah. But if you're going to go anyway, get me some honey. They have the best in the world and it's good for when you're sick."

"Honey?"

"Yes, honey. As long as you make it back alive."

A few days later, I hopped on a bus a few blocks from the Seminary and started backpacking through Yemen.

The only preparation I had made was to buy a ticket for the two-day bus trip through Salalah in southern Oman and into Seiyun, the first major city across the Oman–Yemen border. I didn't have any hotel reservations, tour guides, or plans for what I would do once I got there, but I knew I would be one of the few Americans to have a visa from the land crossing between Yemen and Oman.

***

Yemen had its own infectious spirit that attacked my senses from the moment I crossed its border. Getting to Yemen was the most important part of the journey because it tricked me into forgetting everything I knew about life outside Yemen. If I had flown into Sana'a, the capital, I would have found myself wandering through a bustling Middle Eastern city with overtones of medieval flair. But I didn't fly into Sana'a; I rode through the desert for almost two days in a forty-passenger bus looking at nothing but brown sand that was empty of people, other roads, cities, and cars. There was nothing to see or experience except sand. My only respite was praying the rosary and listening to the Qur'an on my iPod.

In the midst of that profound nothingness, about ten hours after we crossed the Yemeni border, we passed a lone child as we slowed down to navigate an unmanned checkpoint. I stared at him through my window as he stared at me from his camel. The desert seemed inhospitable to any life, much less human life, so it was a shock to see that boy staring back at me. As we continued to drive, I could see a small collection of houses that seemed to be perched on the edge of a precipice that I assumed was that boy's home. It all felt like a dream because it was so out of place. When those images were quickly replaced with more endless sand, I wondered if that boy and cluster of homes were just a mirage, a trick my mind played on me to fill my brain with traces of humanity. Moments later as I stared off into new flecks of brown sand, I doubted his existence.

I was traveling through a place I had read about since I had started at the University of Chicago—Rub' al-khālī, the Empty Quarter. I finally understood how it had gotten that name. Travelers like me were left with nothing but their thoughts; it was a visual emptiness that created an emptiness in the mind and spirit. I ran out of things to think about and be afraid of—I forgot Abdullah's impassioned warnings. At the monastery I had filled my mind with the Psalms and working in the bakery, but in the desert I ran out of things to distract me and simply stared out the window, consumed by a sense of detachment from any other life I had known. It was one of the most intoxicating experiences I had ever had. Yemen enveloped me in itself.

After forty hours of driving through the Omani and Yemeni deserts, I knew that something was happening when the bus started to tilt its way up and down long, winding, narrow hills. The effect of changing elevation added a variation to our unending flat, slow trudge and signaled that we were nearing the end of our journey. By the time we pulled into the bus station in Seiyun, everyone on the bus was bubbling with energy. I had been so deprived of any sort of civilization for two days that I was excited to see people and restaurants in the local square where the bus came to its final stop. I should have been cautious and nervous about being in a country that was best known for growing terrorists and kidnapping foreigners, but I had been sucked into the spirit of Yemen. I didn't care that there were men walking around in traditional garb with knives at their side; I just wanted to get out.

As my fellow travelers and I descended from the bus, we were immediately swarmed by taxi drivers looking to make money. I was wearing khaki pants with a button-down shirt and wondered whether the taxi drivers would recognize me as a foreigner and charge me exorbitant prices. I was nervous in a way that felt completely comfortable. It was the summer of 2006, and I had been on so many buses, taxis, and airplanes in Egypt and Oman that I was used to being uncomfortable and excited at the same time.

Thankfully, I was attacked with the same vigor as the rest of the travelers and participated in the same ritual of rejecting the first few taxi drivers so everyone would know that I was haggling for a good price. But I was just acting. Unlike my travel companions who were headed home from places like Dubai and Bahrain, I had no idea where I was going or what I was doing.

After a few tense discussions, a short, stocky taxi driver casually walked up to me with a big smile and asked, "Wayn b-ruh, akhī?" (Where are you going, brother?)

My initial reaction was to brush him away, but I got a feeling that he wasn't treating me like a foreigner. I asked, "B-t'arif 'an fundūq?" (Do you know of any hotels?)

"Na'am. Yallah." (Yes, let's go.)

I immediately trusted this guy. For some reason, I had no doubts about his intentions and hopped into the front seat of his taxi.

As soon as he shut his door, he asked me the question I knew was coming. "Min wayn anta, a<u>kh</u>ī?" (Where are you from, my brother?)

My charade never worked for very long. I could easily get along speaking Arabic, but like most foreign language students, I pronounced words in a way that revealed Arabic was not my first language. No one ever thought that I was American, but they knew I wasn't an Arab.

"Ana Amrīkī. Min wayn anta?" (I'm American. Where are you from?)

"Haqqan?" (Really?)

We both laughed at my ridiculous question, but it was my way of connecting, and it worked.

"Ana min henna, Yemen." (I'm from here, Yemen.)

After we talked about Chicago for a few moments, my driver, Attalluh, took me to a clean hotel and insisted that he show me the sites around Seiyun. I agreed, and the next morning Attalluh knocked on my door at 8:00 a.m. with a stone-faced expression and began by speaking to me in Arabic, asking me where I wanted to go that day and, when I couldn't give him an answer, telling me he'd find something.

He started off by taking me to his favorite restaurant, where we had fūl and eggs, before he took me to see the Kathiri Palace, an amazing residence that looked like a Benedictine monastery built out of desert sand.

Attalluh and I spent the next few days becoming friends; he took me around Seiyun and the neighboring cities of Tarim and Shibam. He exuded confidence and kindness without saying much. Unlike some of the other taxi drivers, he didn't smile nonsensically at me to get a bigger tip. I felt like I was his friend, and it seemed he was doing everything he could to help me understand his culture. I was paying for his time, but he wasn't trying to take advantage of me.

Day after day, he picked me up in the morning and ate breakfast with me, and then we spent the afternoons crawling around ancient rubble before settling down to a late dinner, where we talked about Yemeni history and customs. I felt comfortable around Attalluh. Not the kind of comfortable discomfort I was used to—I was actually comfortable.

My time with fundamentalists—even Abed and Abdullah— always had a sense of discomfort to it. They were serious, proper types who I could tell were judging me depending on how I pronounced this or that word. But Attalluh was just a regular guy in his late twenties—he knew less about the Qur'an and Islamic theology than I did, so we bonded on a different level. A normal level. I learned from Attalluh by just being with him—hanging out with him and his friends until late in the evening taught me something about the Middle East that I couldn't have gotten anywhere else. I heard them talking about the same things I talked about with my friends: how the day went, who was being an asshole, and family drama. My transition to being fully steeped in Islamic culture had already happened, but I was being introduced to the life of normal, everyday people.

After spending close to two weeks in Seiyun, I told Attalluh it was time for me to see more of Yemen. He asked me a question I didn't expect: "Which route do you want to take?"

"I have no idea. How many routes are there?"

"I like the northern route because it takes you through Ma'rib and then Sana'a before you turn south and head to 'Aden."

"That sounds good to me. How do I get a ticket?"

For a long moment, Attalluh just looked at me. We had been speaking Arabic until he broke our flow with this uncomfortable pause.

"Brother!" Attalluh exhaled, the word emerging from his subconscious in a sincere moment of exasperation. "You're not Yemeni. You can't take the northern route."

For another long moment, we both stared at each other, confused. I sipped my tea while he chewed on his qat—a mild hallucinogen that Yemeni men stuff in their cheeks and lie around enjoying for much of the afternoon.

"You can't go that way. The northern route goes through a terrorist stronghold, and foreigners aren't allowed to travel that way."

I could read the look on Attalluh's face; he'd forgotten that I wasn't Yemeni, and I knew immediately that I had to take the northern route.

"I'll go."

Ma'rib was one of the most famous locations in Middle Eastern history because the biblical Queen of Sheba had lived there. I hadn't imagined that I'd have the chance to visit, but when Attalluh mentioned it, I knew we had to try.

I confirmed my choice, "I don't want to take the southern route. I want to go through Ma'rib."

Attalluh grabbed me by the arm. "Let's go."

As we raced through the streets of Seiyun, Attalluh told me that his dad was the chief of police and he would see what he could do to help me travel through the North. When we finally got to the police station, Attallah pushed me past the security inspections and sat me down in a small room with a bunch of police officers sitting around chewing qat.

Attalluh's dad was the center of attention. Everyone was trying to get his attention or impress him with some information they had picked up on their patrols. Attalluh and I sat there for a moment until his father turned to us and said, "Yes, my son?"

That was the only part of the conversation I understood. Attalluh and his father spoke quickly and in hushed tones. Every so often, someone would look me up and down and shake their head in sur-prise or disappointment. Attalluh was my lawyer, and I was asking the chief of police if I could break the law by taking the northern route to Sana'a. Whatever Attalluh said must have worked because after a few rounds of disagreement, his dad summoned one of the younger officers and signed a piece of paper. Attalluh quickly whisked me off to the bus station to buy a ticket for that evening.

I couldn't believe my luck in having befriended the son of the police chief. It seemed like just yesterday that I had gotten off the bus in Seiyun and encountered Yemen for the first time; and now I was on my way through a dangerous part of the country. I waved goodbye to Attalluh and promised him that I would stop in Seiyun on my way back to Oman.

I never saw him again.

***

At the first checkpoint, which was meant to deter the smuggling of guns and terrorists, a young soldier wearing a uniform that was two sizes too big slowly climbed up the stairs to the bus and called out, "Where's the American?"

I was shocked. I wondered whether he was talking about me.

Of course he's talking about me. How did he know I was on the bus? Did the police chief rat me out?

I was motionless.

The other passengers on the bus were more confused than me and answered, "There are no Americans on here!"

One of them dismissed the young soldier's question and another made a loud joke, saying, "Here I am!"

The officer lost his nerve, fumbled his way off the bus, and disappeared into their makeshift stone office building in the middle of nowhere, Yemen. We all waited and everyone else chatted about how ridiculous that officer had been when an older, fatter officer stormed on the bus, shouting, "Where is the American?"

By then I was prepared to answer. "Here."

Everyone on the bus craned their necks to see me slowly raising my hand.

"Bring me your passport!"

I got up as quickly as I could but barely forced my legs to make the long trek down the aisle of that bus before he snatched the passport from my hand and stormed off. I had been stripped of my most valuable possession and didn't know whether I should return to my seat or stand there with dozens of eyes boring holes in my back. My passport was my only connection to the outside world. No one knew where I was, and my only hope, if I got lost, ran out of money, or was kidnapped was that my blue passport would get me out of trouble. I could hear Abdullah saying, *They kidnap foreigners for fun!*

As my feet grew roots into the floor of that bus, the other passengers grew angrier with the unexpected delay. Finally, the older man returned and thrust the passport back into my hand. I dropped my head and lumbered my way back to my seat, hoping there would be no more delays.

The police chief had indeed phoned ahead—because he wanted to make sure I didn't disappear along the way. Unfortunately, I was called to the front of the bus at every checkpoint, and by the fourth time, the men on the bus had had enough of the delays and started interrogating me.

"What are you doing in Yemen?"

"I've heard so much about how beautiful Yemen is that I had to see it for myself."

"Are you Muslim?"

"No, I'm Catholic."

"Do you work for the CIA? Is that why you are in Yemen?"

The tone of the questions had turned hostile.

"No. I'm a student."

"Where are you a student?"

"In Chicago."

As the bus rolled down the road, different men were firing questions in my direction, and I was having trouble figuring out how to respond. When I spoke Arabic one-on-one, I knew how to crack a joke at the right point to break the tension, but I was completely surrounded and the questions just kept coming. I could see people in the front of the bus shaking their heads as I stuttered to explain myself. All of the knowledge I had about Islam slipped out of my head. All of the arguments I had developed for why US policy could be fixed and how we could partner with Muslim countries escaped my tongue. My trepidation emboldened them and brought more people to the conversation.

It was in that moment that I first experienced being on the receiving end of the deep suspicion that people all over the Middle East had for the CIA. Everywhere I went, people thought it was ridiculous that a tall Black man could be from the United States, and if they did believe I was American, then I had to be a CIA spy. If I had not been living my life as an experiment to solve US–Middle Eastern relations, I would have just lied and said I was from Kenya and my native language was Swahili—or English. No matter where I went, though, I forced myself to experience the biases of fundamentalists and everyday Arabs. It was a painful but necessary exercise if I wanted to have the influence over policy that I thought I deserved.

Just as the men started to really organize against me, the bus driver pulled over at a convenience store on the side of the road in the middle of the empty desert. In an instant I stopped being the most important distraction from the emptiness of the Yemeni desert and we all filed out of the bus. It was a small one-story building painted immaculately white on the outside but miserably dirty on the inside. There were metal plates on the counter with cooked chickens for travelers who needed a quick snack before they hurried back to their nothingness. I had no idea how long those chickens had been there, but I got in line like everyone else and held my plate out as the man behind the counter slopped rice and tomato sauce on it. Once we paid, everyone sat on the benches together outside. Except me—I ate inside the store, hoping to put some distance between me and my interrogators.

I wanted to run. Or hail a cab and make a mad dash back to Oman, but we were in the middle of the desert. There was nothing as far as the eye could see except that store and an infinity of brown sand. I didn't have any choice but to wash down cold chicken and rice with an Orange Fanta and wait for the moment that my stomach turned against me. When the men started filing back on the bus, I prepared for another round of assaults for the next five hours of our trip. Once everyone had piled into the bus, a man sat down beside me. My initial reaction of instant terror was replaced with curiosity.

"Min wayn anta, a<u>kh</u>ī?" he asked. (Where are you from, my brother?)

"The US."

"I think we all know that you're from the US, but where in the US?"

He had awkwardly turned his body so he could look directly at me as we sat on the same narrow seat.

"I live in Chicago. That's where I go to school."

"Oooohhhh…Chicago. That's where the mob is, right? Bang! Bang!"

He laughed; I held my breath. I didn't know where this conversation about the mob and guns was going.

"…Yes. There used to be a lot of mobsters in Chicago, but not so much anymore."

"Oh, really? What's it like there?"

He asked me about Norristown, my family, and my studies in Chicago. He told me about his hometown of 'Amran, how difficult it was to get diabetes medication in Yemen, and how he wished he didn't have to work in the Gulf and spend so much time away from his family.

For the first hour, I expected him to reach out at any moment and slice my neck open with the khanjar knife hanging at his side; but the longer we talked, the more the other men on the bus learned about me. I stopped being an American that was the embodiment of their xenophobia and became a human being with a story that made sense to them. One man asked about racism in America. Another asked about my time in Oman. They all took the time to tell me about their villages and invited me to have dinner with their families. As their fascination with the CIA receded, we recreated a ritual that happens on planes, trains, and buses all over the world—we got to know one another as if we would see each other again.

The rest of the bus trip was a crash course in Yemeni culture and history. The men stopped accusing me of destabilizing their country and spent time trying to explain how tribal and religious differences boiled over into violence in their country. They described vast areas of their country where the government had no presence and terrorists built training camps where people learned how to blow themselves up in other countries.

Ma'rib was a complete letdown because we drove through in the middle of the night, but the education I received from those men helped me understand how non-fundamentalists understood the role of fundamentalists in their religion and country. They felt helpless. Most of the men were traveling home from their jobs in other countries because they couldn't find work in Yemen. They wished they could change the future of their country, but they were too busy trying to provide for their families. They were afraid of terrorists who gave their country a bad name, but they didn't believe they had any power to make a difference.

***

My first two weeks in Yemen set the pattern for the rest of my trip. In Sana'a, a taxi driver took me to the Sindbad Hotel and spent days showing me the Old City, explaining its geometric architecture and discussing Yemeni culture with me. In 'Aden, the owner of a fleabag hotel I discovered while wandering the streets made sure I found the only place to drink beer and protected me from the police. Everywhere I went, in al-Hudaydah, Ta'izz, and Mukalla, the experience was the same. The Yemenis I met were wary of foreigners, but the moment I spoke Arabic with them and shared the story of my life, they showed me the greatest hospitality. Abdullah had warned me about Yemenis, but my experience was completely different.

Over the course of more than a month, I crawled through every major city, learning about one of the oldest civilizations in the world.

When I made it to Makalla, a picturesque city in eastern Yemen with a river bisecting its downtown, I decided it was time to go home. I was hurtling through the darkened streets of downtown on the back of a motorcycle with no helmet or regard for my life when it dawned on me that I was truly getting sucked into Yemen. I had spent the past few days subconsciously making plans to lock myself away in an apartment where I could study with a local imām and hang out with Yemenis at night. It would have been a perfect mash-up of the extreme and the everyday. In some fantastical way, I had forgotten about my PhD and was consumed by a new life of deep connection and personal fulfillment that came from living with people who took the time to share themselves and allowed me to be me.

I had met the driver of that motorcycle, Yasīn, when he was my waiter a week earlier. We spent most of every day talking about Indian Ocean trade routes and the nights listening to his friends dream about building a house and getting married. When we arrived at my hotel that night and Yasīn throttled down, I got off my first ever motorcycle ride and told him that it was time for me to go back to Chicago. I felt like I needed to say it out loud before my new reality completely consumed my consciousness.

He begged me to stay. "So soon? You've barely seen anything."

"Yasīn, akhī, you've been too kind to me. If I stay, I'll have to give you my sister's hand in marriage to pay you back."

We both laughed, and he put his arm around my shoulder.

"I've never had an akhī from America. Will you email me when you get back to America? Maybe I will come visit you."

"Email? I have your phone number. I'll call you as soon as I get back to Oman."

When he knocked on my hotel door the next morning, I had bad news for him. "Yasīn, the police came to my room this morning and said that I can't take the bus to Seiyun. Did you tell them about me?"

"Of course not! I would never do that. Wait here."

Yasīn disappeared for a few minutes and returned in a rush, asking, "Are you packed?"

"Yes, why?"

"Let's go. Quickly!"

Yasīn snatched my backpack, grabbed me by the hand, and pulled me down the stairs. When we made it outside, he ran out in front of a taxi and ordered me inside.

"Yasīn! What's going on?"

I was worried we were going to make a run for the bus station and get shot down by the police.

"The idiot at the front desk told the police about you, and now they are saying you need to pay for a military escort to Seiyun."

"What! Where are we going?"

"The general is my uncle; we're going to talk to him."

Once again, I couldn't believe my luck.

When we got to the front gate of the military base, Yasīn told the taxi driver to wait and pushed his way through the guards. I had less than an hour before the last bus was leaving, and Yasīn started talking as soon as he sat on the floor with the rest of the soldiers. The general was annoyed.

"Foreigners aren't allowed to travel from here to Seiyun! It's too dangerous. He'll need to pay for a military escort."

"Uncle. Please listen to me. Alexander is not a foreigner. Please look at him; he looks like one of us and he is a good man. I consider him my a<u>kh</u>ī."

At the word *a<u>kh</u>ī*, the General looked at me and asked, "Why are you in Yemen?"

Yasīn's urgency had already infected me, and I implored the general with my eyes and words. I knew flattery was usually the best tactic.

"I came to learn more about your country. I heard that the people were more hospitable than anyone else in the world and speak the best Arabic." I didn't tell him what Abdullah said.

The general looked around the room at the soldiers sitting with us. Everyone nodded their heads in agreement with my assessment of the Yemeni people.

"Please, Uncle. He already traveled from Seiyun all the way through the country. He has permission from the police chief in Seiyun. He'll be fine."

The general waved Yasīn over and they talked in hushed tones before Yasīn grabbed a piece of paper from the general, hopped up, and whisked me off the base and down to the bus station. After we secured my seat, I turned and thanked Yasīn.

"You're welcome."

I thanked him profusely, but he just stood there, staring at me.

"It's going to be expensive."

"What do you mean?" I was stalling. I only had a few minutes before the bus was leaving, and I knew exactly what Yasīn meant.

"The general expects something for letting you go."

I fished around in my pocket and slowly pulled out a $20 dollar bill.

"Do you have anything else?"

I didn't have time to argue, so I gave Yasīn all the money in my pockets and one of the emergency stashes I had in the bottom of my backpack. Giving him stacks of cash was a better option than paying for an armored convoy like the general wanted. Yasīn was finally satisfied with the money I was thrusting in his hand, we hugged, and I hopped on the bus just as the driver started pulling out of the station.

By the time I got back to Oman, I had missed Attalluh in Seiyun and found Abdullah's honey spilled all over my backpack; I was ready to be back in Chicago. I didn't know that Yemen was my final preparation for combat.

Part Three:
A War Story

Preparing for Combat

When I got back to Chicago in September, the only thing on my mind was getting my PhD so I could finally get a job fixing US policy. After finishing my master's degree, I was expected to take one or two years of classes before sitting for a grueling academic exercise. Qualifying examinations consisted of four written tests given on four separate days in which I would walk into the front office and get a single piece of paper in a sealed envelope. That piece of paper would have one or more questions, and I'd have four hours to write a twenty-five-page response. Each exam was based on a different set of thirty books that I had to cite from memory. There was a free day between each exam, and after they were all completed, I had to take an oral examination, during which my professors could ask me questions from any of 120 books or anything else they thought I should know.

There were always rumors going around that it was impossible to fail qualifying exams, but I knew someone who had failed the previous year, and that scared me into the library for hours every day. Failing meant that you would be kicked out of the program and probably never find a school that would let you finish your PhD. I moved out of Lesia's house and locked myself off from the world so I could study full-time. If I wasn't at the Regenstein Library surrounded by piles of books, I was sitting on my living room floor mapping out theories of human behavior or mumbling my way through the Qur'an while eating dinner at Salonica. I thought I had everything figured out until I got an email that changed the course of my life. I stared at my computer screen in disbelief.

> *We are looking for individuals with advanced degrees in anthropology, sociology, religion, and/or linguistics to help deployed military units understand the socio-political nuances of communities in Iraq and Afghanistan.... You would be part of a new exciting Human Terrain Program that will help redefine the future of US policy.... Applicants should have knowledge of Arabic, Persian, or Dari and have traveled extensively in the region.*

The email was from Michael Mayer at BAE, a British defense contractor whose US subsidiary made airplanes for the Pentagon. The letter ended with these questions: "Are you passionate about the Middle East? Do you want to make a difference in the real world? Why not give me a call so we can chat?"

The email made too much sense to be real, so I sat there trying to figure out which of my friends was pranking me. They were all upset that I'd locked myself away for months since I had gotten back from Yemen, and I assumed that if I dialed the number on the email, it would be one of them waiting for me at the bar. My first guess of the culprit was JJ, so I dialed his number and launched into an accusation: "Haha. Real funny, JJ."

"Alexs?"

"Yeah. I know it was you, JJ. Why are you screwing with me?"

"What are you talking about?"

"I saw the email you sent me. That wasn't funny."

"What email? I didn't send you an email."

Once I realized it wasn't JJ, I called a few other friends. Pauly hung up, and Tommy started yelling at me. After the fifth call, I started to think that maybe the email was legitimate. When I got off the phone with Joey, I reread the email, thinking, *It's just too good to be true.*

I didn't know what else to do, so I emailed Michael Mayer and told him I wanted to learn more about the Human Terrain Program. I received a reply within a few minutes, and he spent the next week explaining that the US Army was sending PhD-level academics to war zones to help the military understand the cultural environments where they operated. It was part of a renewed effort to fully implement counterinsurgency (COIN) policies. The authors of COIN, like General David Petraeus and General Stanley McChrystal, knew that the wars in Iraq and Afghanistan would never be won with bullets and bombs and that anyone associated with the military needed to see themselves as cultural ambassadors first and combatants second. The answer to terrorism wasn't the elimination of terrorists; it was the empowerment of average citizens so that they had the space they needed to stand up to violent instability and create a new society.

Michael Mayer had me hook, line, and sinker. I thought about the brothers at the Institute and the men on the bus to Sanaʻa—about how the best method for improving US–Middle Eastern policies was creating meaningful relationships with normal, everyday Arabs. This was exactly what I had been training for—the reason I abandoned people who cared about me and never hesitated to go where I could learn about fundamentalists. This was the job I needed to fix US policy.

If I took the job with BAE, I would be fully embedded with a military unit in Iraq, but my paycheck would come from BAE. My title would be social scientist and my job would be to design anthropological research that helped the military better understand Iraqis. To prepare for my deployment, I had to spend six months learning about combat anthropology, military operations, and data analysis at Fort Leavenworth near Kansas City. When Mayer and I talked on the phone, I asked all the questions that were burning inside me.

"Where will I live?" I asked him. "How much will I be paid? What kind of danger will I be in? Will I carry a gun? How long will I be overseas?"

"You wouldn't be carrying a gun because you need to create relationships of trust with the locals. You would live with infantry units on military bases, and they will protect you. I'm not ready to talk salary, but the positions are well paid."

I spent two weeks trying to decide if I wanted to go to war, and I remembered one of the things Jean Bethke Elshtain had said in her class on Just War Theory at the University of Chicago:

One of the things many people forget is that there's a moral distinction between why a state goes to war, jus ad bellum, *and how that state conducts the war,* jus in bello. *In an ideal case, a state would only initiate war based on proper justification, but even when it doesn't, there is still a moral obligation to conduct the war in a just way.*

The state, and most importantly, its people, have an obligation to be critical of every step of the process. It's not good enough to shrug your shoulders and say:

"It's not my problem, I didn't want to go to war anyway."

No. If you disagree with the war in Iraq or Afghanistan, it doesn't relieve us of the moral obligation to ensure that the way we conduct the war is just. We're not off the hook yet.

I went back and forth in my mind for weeks and finally made my decision while I was house sitting for Marvin Wilde. I was in the attic where Marvin kept his only television, watching *Iraq for Sale: The War Profiteers*. It described in harrowing detail how KBR, a company that was tied to Vice President Dick Cheney, knowingly sent truck drivers on dangerous routes where they were being killed, even though no goods were being picked up or delivered. Those drivers were getting blown up and dying so that KBR could bill the US government for their time. They weren't dying to save lives or fix US policies; they were dying because of greed.

It was one of the vilest and most disturbing things I had ever heard of: a company profiting off of war so blatantly and with such horrible consequences. Part of me wanted to shut off the television and pretend I had never heard of Iraq, to rush back home and drag my fingers across the pages of the Qur'an until I graduated. But there was a nagging voice in my belly that piped up and screamed at me, *You have to do something about this.*

It wasn't a quiet, consoling voice. It was a deep, moving force that compelled me to make a decision. It wasn't a sense that I *wanted* to act but that I *needed* to act. The choice became simple: I could spend the next two years finishing my dissertation and trying to find a teaching job, or I could do the thing I had wanted to do since 9/11 happened. That voice immediately started working on my need to always follow my passion: *This is your chance to make a difference. If things are that bad, you have to do something about it. You can make a real difference. Besides, it's only one year, and it will be great experience for future jobs.*

I picked up my phone, called Michael Mayer, and uttered the phrase that had become a defining fixture of my life: "I'll go."

I told only a few people. Students and professors at the University of Chicago were split over whether we should have invaded Iraq. There were professors in the economics and political science departments who had advised President George W. Bush and proudly supported the Iraq War. Some of my friends agreed and thought that the war would bring about fundamental changes the Middle East needed. In reality, though, there was only one person whose opinion mattered to me: Marvin Wilde.

Marvin and I had grown close throughout my time at the University of Chicago, and he took every chance to force me to think through the most difficult problems in philosophy and religion; he became my doktorvater, my academic father. He didn't force me to study or believe any one thing; he just challenged me to expand my brain until it felt like it might crack. I trusted him implicitly, and he rewarded me with unfettered access to his time and brilliance.

He had an entirely different reputation in the Divinity School. He was an unforgiving critic and regularly gave people failing grades, something that was unheard of in graduate school. He publicly challenged his colleagues and intimidated anyone who got in his way. Most importantly, Marvin was completely against the war and wrote a book denouncing Bush's decision. Marvin considered it an unjust war and believed that the only reason we went to war in Iraq was to get access to the country's oil reserves. At the height of things, he was arrested while leading a protest in downtown Chicago.

Rather than get caught up in never-ending and vitriolic political discussions, I told Marvin and almost everyone else that I would spend the next year traveling in the Middle East doing research. My passion to save the world propelled me into my next adventure, and a week after I passed my qualifying exams, I was on a plane to Fort Leavenworth. I didn't know that the vitriol I had hoped to avoid would be directed at me just one year later.

***

When I landed in Kansas City, I expected to enter an environment like that of grad school, but on our first day, the soldiers and civilians running the Human Terrain Program were so unprepared that they gave us lessons in how to do Internet searches. After experiencing a full week of complete disorganization, one other guy and I started taking three-hour lunches. Brian was a former Special Forces soldier, a Green Beret who had gotten out of the Army a few years earlier. We hit it off right away. He was a farm boy from rural Ohio and the first American I had ever met who instinctively believed that war was the best way to make the world a better place. He had joined the Army because he wanted to kill bad guys and give oppressed people a chance for a better life. It's the motto of US Army Special Forces—*De oppresso liber*—to liberate the oppressed—and Brian took it literally. When he joined the Army, he hoped that he would be going into the worst places in the world to help people fight despotic rulers and create a better society.

Brian and I were sitting at a two-person booth at Homer's Drive Inn near Fort Leavenworth when we really started getting to know each other. I asked him, "Why did you leave the Army if you like shooting people so much?"

Brian smiled at me and pushed his French fries around the plate. "Well, I thought that being a trigger puller would get rid of bad guys, but the longer I stayed in, the more idiot officers I had.

"They didn't care about their soldiers or making the world a better place; they just cared about making rank. I saw some fucked-up shit and I couldn't take it anymore."

"So you got out?"

"Ha!" Brian always smiled when he talked about things he didn't want to. "Yeah, it was a great idea; that's why I'm at Leavenworth headed to another shithole.... Well, I guess it's better than working in a windowless cubicle in D.C. trying to figure out how to strangle myself with my phone cord."

"We're gonna make a difference in Iraq, Brian. I know that for a fact."

"Yeah. Sure. I've heard that before."

Brian and I didn't agree on much of anything, and we quickly built a friendship based on our differences. I was fascinated by someone who had traveled the globe with the intention of shooting people to make the world a better place. He couldn't believe I was so naive.

"Let me guess, Alexs. You grew up in a rich family, your parents were academics or doctors or something, and that's why you went to graduate school? You want to *save the world*."

It was more an accusation than a description.

"No way. Are you kidding? What makes you say that?"

"Look at you. You're getting your PhD…"

He curled his fingers in quotes and said *PhD* in a mocking tone.

"…you speak all these languages and act like you're gonna save the world. That sounds to me like someone who hasn't seen the real world."

"Fuck you, Brian. You don't know me."

I was only a little angry, but I was so curious about how he saw the world that I suspended my anger. "It's not that I haven't seen shit. I just don't let what's going on out there define what's going on in here."

I pointed to my head and my chest.

Brian threw his head back and laughed at me.

It was the first time I realized that I was a different Alexs Thompson. People who didn't know my story thought I was successful. Growing up, I was Barry's kid and I deserved pity; I'll never forget the searing compassion from the neighbors who could hear my muffled screams from the basement. For so long, the defining moment of my life was the day my mom married Barry, and it now dawned on me, as I sat in that greasy spoon playing hooky from work, that I was a graduate student, someone who was judged by my brain. People like Brian could never really understand me until they understood my journey.

In the next few moments of silence—while we finished eating and figured out if we could be friends—I began to reassess my own life and had a shocking realization: that scared kid didn't exist anymore.

Barry didn't matter.

I mattered.

I had already become the hero of my life.

Both Brian and I had spent so much time around people who were similar to us that it excited us to know someone different. He refused to believe my stories about Abed in Alexandria and backpacking through Yemen. He had spent plenty of time in the Middle East, but it was always with heavily armed military units that had airplanes flying overhead to protect them. To Brian, I wasn't just a graduate student; I was a crazy adventurer who went to places even he wouldn't go. The more we talked, though, the more he learned about the Middle East and fundamentalists from my perspective. He also learned about my childhood and the choices I had made to create a life that was unthinkable compared to when I lived in Norristown. Over the next few weeks, we became best friends.

We would skip out of the office around lunchtime and sit around talking until the only thing to do was to go to the bar. Surprisingly, the more Brian talked about joining the Army, the more I heard myself in his words: "What else was I going to do? Sit around in Ohio and farm for the rest of my life? I can do that when I'm old. I wanted to fix shit out there. You know what I mean?"

We were sitting at the bar again.

"I know exactly what you mean. I could be in Norristown not doing anything with my life or stuck in the library studying ancient Arabic texts, but I want to make a real difference."

Brian put his arm around my shoulder, laughing. "You're one weird dude! Arabic texts? What are you talking about?"

"Screw you."

We sat there for a moment with Brian grinning into his beer. Then he looked at me with deep concern. "It doesn't get better, Alexs."

"What do you mean?"

"I used to be like you. Well, not that weird, but I was gonna change the world. But it doesn't work. Now I'm just trying to get rich."

"Yeah, right. You still care and you know it."

"Fuck that. We're so fucked it's not even funny. It doesn't matter how much you care or how many people you try to help. The military is gonna screw everything up, and you'll be stuck there with your dick in your hand wondering whether it was all worth it. All the destruction. The time away. Was it really worth it?"

Brian was smiling again.

I couldn't believe him. I lived a life forcefully detached from everyday reality. All of my adventures gave me a chance to run away from the boring, mundane parts of life and construct my own reality that conformed to my perception of myself. I knew that I could change US–Middle Eastern relations because I had put in the time and energy to become a real expert.

We sat there with Brian's arm around my shoulder for a long moment. He was drunk. I was energized. Since 9/11, I had been talking about *my* mission to understand Islamic fundamentalism, but Brian talked about *the* mission. In spite of his cynicism, he helped me realize that there was a mission out there greater than myself. In the beginning, Brian hadn't been motivated to get a job; he'd been motivated by the mission of the Special Forces to bring democracy and freedom to oppressed people. At some point, he started to question his orders and wondered whether the people in charge really knew how to make the world a better place. Ultimately, his dream of saving the world was beaten out of him after a decade of deployments to war zones.

Brian was normally a freewheeling, thoughtless meathead who was quick with a joke, but whenever I asked him about where he'd been and what he'd done, he suddenly looked like he was trying to solve a calculus problem. He struggled to come up with an answer and always shut down the conversation to get back to talking about beer and women. Brian couldn't believe in the mission anymore, and he didn't have anything to replace it with. He went to war to free the oppressed and wound up a victim of his own idealism.

At the time, I told Brian that he was *personally* called to change the world whether everyone else lived up to the task or not. I couldn't wait to spend the next few months—that turned into years—reminding him that the everyday life is a training ground for us to become the hero of our own story. What I didn't realize was that when I hit my ten-year anniversary, I would be just as broken.

***

I didn't meet anyone who shared my hope for the future of US policy until Nicole Suveges joined the program about three months after me. Nicole was a big, bubbly extrovert with crazy red hair that flopped around whenever she started laughing, and she loved to laugh with anyone who would talk to her. It didn't take her long to realize that the people running our program didn't know what they were doing, and she wasn't shy about sharing her opinion.

"One of the people in my class was talking about interviewing prisoners. I couldn't believe it! You can't interview prisoners unless you have special permission and a damned good reason! You can't just walk into a prison with an armed guard behind you and expect an inmate to give you reliable information. Even if he does tell you the truth, you'll never know!"

Before I could agree, Nicole continued, "I know undergraduates who could teach anthropology better than these people. What the hell did we get ourselves into?"

"I know what you mean," I said. "I'm just hoping that once we get to Iraq, we'll be set loose to do our own thing and not have to worry about the nonsense here."

"Yeah, but what about all these other people? We might know what we're doing, but do you think these people are going to be any use to the military?"

"I really don't care, Nicole. I know what I'm going to do when I get there, and that's all that matters."

"What are you going to do?"

"Well…I…have no idea what we're going to do…"

We both laughed as I continued, "…but I know I'm not going to be as bad as the other people here."

I felt comfortable talking to Nicole, but it wasn't until we went for drinks at The Depot after class that I realized how much we had in common.

"I finished my qualifying exams at Johns Hopkins University over a year ago and…I want to get my PhD, but…I don't know. Some things just didn't feel right, so I was going to take a year off when Michael Mayer emailed me."

"That's funny, he emailed me while I was studying for my qualifying exams."

"What did you think when you read the email?" She asked. "I was shocked the military was doing something like this. Now I realize how screwed up it is."

"I was shocked too, but I knew it was what I wanted to do."

"Right away? It took me a while to convince my family that I wanted to do it."

"Right away. It took me a while to admit it, but I knew I was going to do it the moment I realized it wasn't a gag email from my buddies."

Nicole was a colleague—someone who had passion and beliefs similar to mine. We could talk for hours—usually when Brian left us alone when he met someone at the bar—about how we were going to change the world.

***

By January 2008, I had developed a comfortable life in Leavenworth. BAE put me up in a furnished two-bedroom condo and paid me more money than I would have made after twenty years teaching at a university. I didn't learn much in my classes, but Brian taught me the operator mindset—how to survive in combat—while Nicole challenged me to stay true to my principles. When I finally got the call from my team leader about our deployment orders, I thought I was ready to go to Iraq. Then I heard, "We're going to Fallujah."

I was silent.

My mind raced to the most vivid image I had of Fallujah: four Blackwater security guards' mutilated bodies hanging from a bridge. I thought about how the Marines had walled off the city and only allowed Iraqis to come and go through gates guarded by Americans. Everything I knew about Fallujah was bad.

"Are you there?" My team leader broke the silence.

"Yeah."

"What are you thinking, Alexs?"

"Well...I'm thinking I want to go get a drink."

"Were you hoping to go to Baghdad?"

"Not really. I guess I just never thought about where we'd be going."

"I know what you mean. I never thought we'd go to Fallujah since there aren't any Army units there, but apparently the Marines decided they needed help, so we'll be the first Human Terrain Team in Fallujah."

"Okay. Have you talked to the rest of the team?"

"Not yet. I wanted to make sure you were on board. We need to make sure the rest of the team knows we're on the same page."

"Yeah. I'll go."

"Good. Now, go get a beer, and we'll tell the rest of the team tomorrow."

Iraq

Our chartered airliner full of soldiers and civilians landed at Baghdad International Airport (BIAP) in the middle of the night in March 2008. We had barely come to a halt on the runway when the airplane lit up with energy. A soldier stormed onto the plane and started yelling, "Let's go, people. It's late and I want to go to bed. Everyone up and out. Let's move."

Another soldier gave us our marching orders once we'd tumbled our way onto the tarmac.

"You *will* form a single file line and you *will* follow me. You will *not* wait for your bags. You will *not* wait for your buddy. You will *not* form a gaggle. You will form a single-file line and you will follow me."

I felt like I was in a bad 1990s boot camp movie.

When I finally got my bearings, I could feel the heat and see the sand, but it didn't feel like the Middle East. People were scurrying around wearing US Army uniforms, yelling in various dialects of English, and I didn't see any Arabic scrawled across the terminal or women wearing traditional Islamic garb. This was not the Middle East I had come to know.

Our soldier-guides marched us off the tarmac and into an outdoor holding area drenched in floodlights, where forklifts eventually delivered our supplies and luggage. As soon as the forklifts backed into the darkness, there was a mad dash as passengers gathered their seabags and identified the rest of their team.

My team leader was Mark Stolt, a major in the Army who had gone to West Point and gotten a master's degree in logistics from MIT. He considered becoming an Army Ranger to be his proudest accomplishment, but he was originally a smart hippie from L.A. who joined the Army to work his body as hard as he worked his mind. Our senior military member was Sergeant Major Bill Nast, who had been in the Army for twenty-five years. For the past few years, he had been taking various reservist jobs around the country to avoid retirement for as long as possible.

We also had two translators, Ali Munir, a US soldier who was Egyptian, and Khadija Majady, an Iraqi American civilian. Ali had joined the Army as an 09L, or "oh-nine-lima," a special program that recruited native speakers of Arabic for the War on Terror. Like all green-card holders, Ali would get his American citizenship in return for his service during combat. Khadija was a fifty-something Iraqi housewife from Detroit who was as afraid of going to Iraq as the rest of us were.

Once we had all of our belongings, Sergeant Major Nast herded us to the office of one of his old Army buddies and secured us housing for the night and transportation to Fallujah in the morning.

When we woke up the next morning, Nast took us out to the same holding area where we had collected our baggage the night before and pushed us into a mini-fleet of Humvees. The trip from Baghdad to Fallujah was a slow, bumpy three-hour ride full of supposed roadside bombs that all turned out to be dead animals or discarded boxes of rotten vegetables.

Once we got to Fallujah, Mark gave us a week to get used to our housing assignments, find the cafeterias, and organize our office space. Camp Fallujah was massive. It was made up of one large base that was connected to South Camp Fallujah and Camp Baharia to the west. A large cafeteria served thousands of people at a time at most hours of the day. I shared a room with Ali in a shipping container turned into an apartment, with two beds, dressers, and free-standing metal closets. The showers and toilets were a five-minute walk through the densely populated residential area. Laundry, Internet, TV, and food were all free.

By the second week, Khadija realized what she had gotten herself into and hopped on the first flight back to Detroit. Around that time, Sergeant Major Nast turned into a dictator. We were sitting in the office when he tried to lay down the law.

"I want everyone lined up outside my room at zero-six-hundred, that's 6:00 a.m. for you, Dr. Thompson. We'll do morning physical training (PT), you'll have thirty minutes for showers, then we'll go to breakfast and then to the office. Lunch is from twelve to thirteen-hundred, 1:00 p.m., and quitting time is seventeen-hundred. Evening PT will start at eighteen-hundred, and you'll be free after dinner until lights out at twenty-two hundred."

No matter how many times I corrected Sergeant Major—he insisted we call him that—he always called me Dr. Thompson.

My response to his list of rules was short: "I'm not doing that."

I turned around and walked out of our office.

By the start of the third week, Mark had befriended the other Marine officers, and our team was invited to the daily regimental meetings where everyone reported on operations from the previous day. Mark was sitting at the table with the rest of the staff when Colonel Facelli, the regimental commander, turned to him.

"So, what is a Human Terrain Team?"

"Sir. The Human Terrain Team is another set of eyes and ears for your area of responsibility. We have a social scientist who is trained in engaging local communities, and we'll work with your Marines to identify fundamental drivers of the insurgency and develop plans to build relationships to address those drivers."

"Who do you work for?"

"Well…"

I could see the wheels turning in Mark's head—how to explain that we were a mixture of military and civilian consultants—so I jumped in. "We work for you, sir. We'll go wherever you need us, whenever you want."

"Who are you?"

"My name is Alexs Thompson, and I'm the social scientist."

The colonel smirked. "Well, okay….a new set of eyes and ears…you work for me…I guess that's all I need. Anyone have anything else?"

No one said anything.

"Okay, you're all dismissed."

I spent the next few weeks going to meetings and interviewing any Marine who would talk to me. I wanted to understand how they were fighting insurgents before I made any suggestions about how they should interact with the people of Fallujah. I learned very quickly that there were a lot of Marines who didn't care about the mission of helping Iraqis rebuild their communities. In one of my first interviews, Gunner Miller made it all sound simple: "Marines like to drink and fuck. If we can't find either, we're gonna fight. And in case you haven't heard, we're not allowed to do the first two while we're in this shithole."

Gunner Miller was a big barrel of a man who commanded the attention of the room with his deep, booming voice. He held the rarest rank in the Marine Corps. "Gunner" is reserved for those who have had a long and prestigious career as an enlisted weapons expert. When a gunner spoke—any gunner—everyone listened, even the officers. Gunner Miller expressed a similar indifference to the mission that I heard from others. Operation Iraqi Freedom wasn't about Iraqis or spreading democracy; it was about a bunch of guys from America who only wanted to go home so they could sleep with their wives.

I thought my perspective might be biased from talking to senior enlisted and Marine officers, so I started talking to junior Marines around Camp Fallujah who spent most of their time out in the neighborhoods interacting with Iraqis. Their perspective was worse.

"I don't know why the fuck we're here!"

"All these fuckers want to blow us up."

"Why are we fighting for these camel jockeys? We're dying over here!"

Fallujah in 2008 wasn't as bad as Fallujah in 2004, but Marines were still dying from IEDs, snipers, and suicide bombers. They were angry because they were confused. They didn't care about foreign policy, and they certainly didn't value the life of everyday Iraqis. They cared that their friends were being killed. Politicians and generals talked about winning hearts and minds, but the Marines talked about killing as many "towelheads" as possible.

The more time I spent patrolling the areas in and around Fallujah, the more I understood the pain of junior Marines. Many of them were uneducated and ill-equipped to be the pointy end of the COIN spear. They didn't take showers for weeks, went without a hot meal for months, and the only way they knew to deal with the death of their friends was to get angry.

When I got back to my office after one of my first trips to the city of Fallujah, I called Nicole to get her opinions. She had been posted to Baghdad.

"It's pretty bad out here in Fallujah. How are things over there?"

"It's going great here. What's wrong in Fallujah?"

I sighed. "Tell me about Baghdad. I need some good news."

"Well, I've been here for just a few weeks, and the military commanders are actually happy to have a woman on the team. They said it's the only way they get to hear about how Iraqi women are being affected by the war. I can go places even the female soldiers can't go and I'm already doing some amazing stuff. Do you have access to our website on SIPR, the classified network? I've posted some reports already." She sounded excited.

"That sounds awesome. You're really doing it, huh? I have SIPR, but I don't think I have access to your portal."

"Now, tell me what you've been doing."

I got right to the point. "I've been interviewing Marines all around Fallujah, and it's pretty obvious that they are the ones who need the most help understanding why we're in Iraq and how to interact with Iraqis. I thought I was going to be here helping Iraqis, but it's painful listening to these young guys struggling with being separated from their families and dealing with their friends dying…"

"That's why we're here, Alexs. We have to figure out how to ease the suffering wherever it is. If you think you can make the biggest difference with the Marines, then focus your energy on them."

Nicole and I talked every week, and she knew just the right thing to say to keep me motivated to carry out my mission.

***

It wasn't until I met Lance Corporal Brown that I saw how I could make a difference. He was an intelligence Marine from the second battalion, third Marines (referred to as "2/3"), and he was obsessed with understanding insurgent networks in and around Fallujah. He spent all of his time poring over maps and classified reporting until he knew everything about the people who were hell-bent on killing Americans.

We were standing over a table in his office that was stacked with maps and crowded on all sides with communications equipment, which was being operated by other Marines trying to deal with the most recent attack in Fallujah. "If you pay attention, it's not that hard to figure out what these guys are going to do. They don't have a lot of options when it comes to routes and munitions, so you can eliminate most things until you only have a couple of options."

"What do you mean?" I asked.

"Well, take these rat lines, for example…"

"Rat lines? What're rat lines?"

Brown pulled a map from one of his desk drawers, snapped it out on the table between us, and pointed out the boldly colored lines. "These are the major routes in and around Fallujah. But do you see these other lines, the thinner ones?"

We were both huddled over the table, dragging our fingers over the faded images. I nodded.

"Okay, those are the ways insurgents avoid our checkpoints and travel through the city. We call them rat lines."

"Why don't you just put up more checkpoints?" It seemed like the obvious thing to do.

"We don't have enough people to man that many checkpoints. Besides, for every checkpoint we would set up…see this point, right here?"

"Yeah."

"Well, even if we set up a checkpoint right there, they'd just alter their routes and we wouldn't be able to monitor their movements. You see—" Brown whirled around and grabbed a stack of reports from another drawer. "—you see all these reports? They come from our surveillance of the rat lines. We get an idea of when people cross, the size of the groups, and what directions they're headed. It didn't make sense to me at first, but it's actually a great way to keep tabs on our environment."

Brown was the first Marine I'd met who was trying to solve a riddle. He wasn't just trying to make it back to California; he wanted to figure out how to make Iraq a safer place. I started visiting Brown every day to learn about how the Marines operated, and eventually he introduced me to other intelligence Marines scattered around the city. There was a deep experience of confusion and anger among the Marines, but the more time I spent outside the safety of Camp Fallujah, the more I learned that there were always people who were more committed to the mission of counterinsurgency than they were to their emotions and discomfort.

Once, we were preparing to go on a patrol through Saqlawiyah, a town northwest of Fallujah, when the Marines realized there were no Iraqi interpreters available. One of the section leaders called for Private First Class Jones and asked him if he could act as interpreter. To my surprise, the short Black kid from the South piped up with a simple but confident "Yes."

The Marines didn't know me well and didn't ask me to help, but I figured if things got too hairy, I could step in and do the translating. We finished our patrol briefing and headed out the front gate on foot. The "interpreter" slung the M249 Squad Automatic Weapon over his shoulder and joked with his buddies in a deep southern accent. After our first interaction with the locals, I was amazed at his abilities. He wasn't fluent in Arabic, but he knew how to navigate his way through pleasantries and basic conversation topics. As soon as he finished, I bombarded him with questions, and he answered them with as much humility and confidence as when he had volunteered for his duties.

"Where did you study Arabic?"

"Well…we didn't really study—we all got a few hours of Arabic in our pre-deployment training—but I just hang out with the interpreters and try to learn as much as I can."

"Really? Did you study a language in college?"

He laughed.

"College? Hell. I barely made it out of high school."

"Really? Where are you from?"

"Oh…I'm from a small town in Georgia; we're not from any big city or anything. Just a small town, really. I wanted to get out and serve my country, but I'm sure I'll wind up back there."

"That's great, Jones. Do you like studying language?"

"Well, I never really thought about it, I guess."

"Well, let me know if you start thinking about going to college. I'll help you if I can."

Jones was a simple kid who poured his life into helping Iraqis. He liked shooting guns as much as the other Marines, but he spent

154

his time in Iraq learning about the people and their language rather than sustaining his anger.

I was starting to understand the Marines in Fallujah. There were pockets of passion that were being overwhelmed by legions of apathy. At the same time that I was learning about Iraqis, I was learning about Marines. I was starting to see that I could have the greatest impact at the intersection of those two groups.

***

It took me a few more weeks to figure out that the Marines had a big problem with religion. The only thing they knew about Islam was that it encouraged people to blow themselves up. They made fun of the women's traditional garb and used the word *hajji*, a term of respect in Arabic, as a religious slur for Iraqi men. The Marines also assumed that religious leaders, or imāms, were the cause of the insurgency in Fallujah and the entire al-Anbar Province. Attitudes about Islam were so confused that the generals in Baghdad had actually forbidden Marines from going to mosques or engaging religious leaders. It was a policy that made sense only if you thought Marines were unteachable and all imāms were out to kill Americans.

I didn't believe either was true.

It was exactly the kind of problem I could fix. After I conducted in-person interviews with the Marines, I started reading classified reporting back to 2003 and found that there had been an effort to do "mosque monitoring," in which American units positioned themselves within earshot of a mosque and recorded the khutba (sermon). In Iraq, like many Muslim countries, the Friday sermon was broadcast from a loudspeaker so everyone in the community could hear it. Those recorded sermons were transcribed by translators working for the US military and stored on various websites on the classified networks. Over the next two weeks, I called every unit that did mosque monitoring and wound up with over 100,000 reports from across the country. Once I had them saved to my hard drive, I developed a process to analyze them all.

First, I read through hundreds of reports from the different units to get an idea of important concepts and locations. Once I understood how the reports were generally organized, I created a new language to code about 100 of those concepts so that the reports could be compared to one another. For example, if a sermon mentioned invaders, the United States, infidels, or any other related words, I coded it as "America." If the report mentioned feeding the poor, helping orphans, or any other related words, I coded it as "Social Responsibility." Once I developed a coding system, I created a process to identify each sermon as positive, neutral, or negative overall. If a sermon mentioned killing Americans or coalition forces, it was negative; but if it mentioned killing insurgents, it was positive. If the sermon was mostly focused on religious issues like prayer and almsgiving, I labeled it neutral. Finally, I labeled each sermon with the name of the imām, the city, the date, and any keywords I found.

My goal was to give the Marines a database from which they could quickly get information they didn't know they needed. For example, a unit could come to me from Ferris Town and ask, "Do you know anything about the religious leaders in our area?"

Or: "I met Muhammad al-Murani. Do you have any info on him?"

Once I had a complete plan, Mark insisted that I get started right away. For the next few weeks, he and I worked twelve-hour shifts, six days a week, to recode the tens of thousands of reports from the city of Fallujah and its suburbs. Our routine was simple. One week, Mark would wake me up at 6:00 a.m. and I would go to the office and start coding reports, only stopping to eat and rest my eyes. At 6:00 p.m., I would wake Mark up and he would work until 6:00 a.m. The next week, after a day of rest, we switched roles and I worked through the night. It became our ritual, and Mark even started listening to

Sa'ad al-Ghamdi's recitation of the Qur'an as a way of getting into the mindset of imāms in Fallujah.

The both of us became immersed in the religion of Islam in Fallujah in a way that no one ever had. When we finished recoding all of the reports, I used geospatial software to build maps that visualized specific neighborhoods and key people and concepts from that area. It was a way for the Marines to better understand the communities where they lived and engage the people in a new way.

The results were surprising. Everyone who heard about our project assumed we would wind up identifying radical clerics that the Marines would go kill, but we found that less than 5 percent of the sermons were hostile to the United States or the coalition, and over 75 percent were neutral. Religious leaders in Fallujah were mostly talking about religious duties like praying and avoiding sin.

I talked a lot about the validity of my results with Nicole. "I know there's bias in our results, considering we're only looking at mosques that had a bunch of Marines waving a recorder around, but do you think we can trust our results?"

"Well, it depends," she mused. "What are you trying to do with your results?"

I kicked back in my office chair and switched the phone from one ear to the other. "I'm trying to help the Marines figure out how to deal with imāms. They think that religious leaders are the root cause of the insurgency, but I don't think they're right, at least not in Fallujah."

Nicole kept pushing me. "Do you think that religious leaders are saying different things in private than they're saying in public?"

"Of course," I said. "We all say different things in public and private. I think the point here is that we don't have any empirical evidence to support the claim that religious leaders are causing the insurgency. And we have a lot of evidence that there are imāms who, week after week, are only talking about religious duties…that might be a pattern we can investigate."

"If I were you, that's how I'd frame it. You haven't proven anything, yet. You've just given the Marines a reason to get to know the religious leaders in their communities."

Nicole hit the nail on the head and gave me the exact language I needed to talk about my findings. Rather than tell the Marines that they were wrong, I identified three religious leaders mentioned in reports from across the Fallujah area who might be good partners in our mission of quelling the insurgency. Once I was convinced of my mission, I started talking about building a religious leader engagement program. It got off to a slow start, but my luck started to change when they realized that my study was based on tens of thousands of sermons by hundreds of imāms. When they saw the depths of the reports I could build, and do so quickly, they finally gave me permission to partner with religious leaders. Marines started coming into our office to search the database, my maps were presented to the colonel, and I was asked to go on more and more patrols across the region.

I was living my kind of life. I had taken an idea of how the world should be, and I had made it a reality.

Addicted to War

My first meeting with an imām didn't go the way I'd hoped. One night, just before nightfall, a company of Marines escorted me through the streets of Fallujah to the house of a local religious leader who had been preaching peace and stability. When we got there, he invited us in, offered us tea, and started yelling at us about a raid that had swept up one of his neighbors. "Why did you attack Muhammad and his family? They are a good family. You claim they are insurgents, but they are not! I know them."

I should have expected him to be hostile; if my research was correct, then this was a man who cared about the spiritual condition of the people in his community, and our actions had hurt them. He wasn't an angry person, but he wanted to protect the people around him. The company commander stepped in and explained why the Marines had conducted a raid in their neighborhood and spent the next hour calming the imām down. I was pushed to the side and never had a chance to talk with him.

Most of my first meetings were derailed by more important issues, and although it was frustrating not talking about religion, I knew my research was helping create deeper relationships and improve stability. Then, one day, a young lance corporal in full battle rattle—bulletproof vest, rifle, and helmet—busted into our office, huffing and puffing with the urgency of a man at war.

"Is there an Alexs Thompson in here?"

I immediately stood up and was infected by this guy's energy.

"We need you right now!" He didn't show any of the normal courtesy to the captain in the office, so I could tell it was urgent.

"Why? What's going on?" I asked.

"There's a bunch of religious leaders getting together, and we heard you know about that shit."

What happened next was one of the most important moments of my life. I felt like Indiana Jones. A nerdy adventurer called into action. I grabbed my helmet and bulletproof vest and ran through Camp Fallujah to a Humvee that whisked me off to the Iraqi countryside.

The imāms at that meeting were from across the area and had taken it upon themselves to figure out how they could work together to fight the insurgency. I recognized their names from the reports I had been writing and inserted myself into the conversation when they started talking about religion. They were all surprised that I knew about the Qur'an and religious law, and by the end of the meeting, I had given my phone number to all of the attendees and promised to visit them in their communities if they were interested.

From that day on, the religious leader engagement program was a success. Once or twice a week, I found myself discussing Islamic theology on my cell phone or at the home of religious leaders in and around Fallujah. I wrote regular reports that were shown to the colonel and his staff and helped them understand which leaders they should engage in the communities around Fallujah. They finally realized that religious leaders were an integral part of the Iraqi cultural fabric.

I had been in Iraq for only three months when I realized that I was having an impact on how the Marines conducted their operations. Things were exceeding my wildest expectations, until one week in June 2008 when my world shattered.

***

I was sitting in my office planning a patrol with Mark for June 24 when he got a call on the office phone. I knew something was wrong when he asked me outside and sat down at the smoke pit right outside of our office. Mark hated smoke, so when he handed me a cigarette that he had gotten from a Marine, I figured it was going to be really bad. It took him a few moments to muster the courage to speak the words he had heard.

"Nicole is dead."

"What?" I stood up.

"Nicole is dead. She was targeted in Sadr City and killed on her way to a meeting with tribal leaders."

My fingers trembled while I tried to light cigarette after borrowed cigarette. I wanted to say something, but I couldn't find the words.

"Are you okay?" Mark tried to get me to talk.

I smiled. I learned that from Brian. It was the first time I really understood that smile.

Mark sat with me for a half hour while I listened to him talk about how war sucks. When I still hadn't said a word, he got up to leave.

"I understand what you're going through. I know you two were close. If you want to talk, let me know. If you want to take a few days off, let me know."

I sat there until the sun started to set, bumming cigarettes off anyone who walked by as if I was a seasoned smoker.

Over the next day, her team gave us more information about how she had died. The terrorists in Sadr City were angry that Nicole was meeting with the community, especially the women. Her bubbly personality meant that even religious leaders, who were all male, felt comfortable interacting with her and talking about resisting terrorist elements. That's why the terrorists killed her, to shut her up and reinforce a culture of fear.

When Mark uttered those words, I felt like a part of my heart had been ripped out. I didn't know how to talk about what I was feeling, so I started replaying our conversations. I reminded myself over and over about a promise Nicole and I had made to one another in Leavenworth: "Well, at least if we die on some dusty Iraqi road, we'll die happy, right?" We would both laugh or clink our beer glasses together. It was more than just a statement; it was an oath that meant we would always put the mission first, even to the point of death.

The Army unit Nicole had worked with started planning a memorial service, and I told Mark I was going to Baghdad.

Two days later, I started hearing rumors about an explosion in Karmah. I was supposed to be at a meeting that day with religious leaders there, but was still processing Nicole's death so I'd skipped it. I ran to the Combat Operations Center (COC), where the regimental staff conducted their work, and yelled at one of my friends, a Marine named McGarrety. He'd been assigned the job of analyzing all of the intelligence that came in from Karmah and explaining it to the senior leadership.

"What happened in Karmah?"

"We're still figuring it out, Mr. Thompson, but there was an explosion."

I had been working closely with McGarrety since I got to Fallujah, and he understood how important it was that we learn how to engage the people of Fallujah. He wasn't pissed off about being in Iraq, and he wasn't just biding his time until he could go home to his family. I had started to train him in basic anthropological theory and how to code reports from Marines in the field. He was smart and we got along great, but I wanted answers.

"McGarrety! What happened?"

He was shocked that I was yelling in the COC and just stood there with his mouth open. The operations officer, the Marine in charge of all the tactical and logistical movements, pulled me aside and uttered three words: "They're all dead."

I was stunned into silence. I wasn't shouting anymore; I was struggling to make sense of what he was telling me. After a long moment, I finally responded, "The Marines or the Iraqis?"

"All of them. The Marines and the Iraqis. Lieutenant Colonel Galeai, Captain Dykeman, and Corporal Preudhomme, along with the Iraqi tribal sheikhs and imāms."

I turned around and ran out of the COC before I could hear any more. I stumbled around the base, trying to force my brain to accept the fact that the meeting I'd helped organize and was supposed to be attending had been blown up. They were all dead, and I was alive.

McGarrety gave me a few minutes alone before he tracked me down and told me the full story. A terrorist cell in Fallujah had found out about the meeting and sent one of their men dressed as an Iraqi police officer to detonate a suicide vest. I had spent a lot of time with almost everyone who died. Weeks earlier, I had talked with Lieutenant Colonel Galeai about including religious leaders in their planning and meetings. Now they were all dead.

Nicole was dead.

As I wandered around in circle after circle through that heavily guarded base, I ran through the images of my friends who were now gone.

The first time I was going to meet Imām Mustafa, for example, I'd told the Marines to find a way to leave me alone with him for a few moments. When they left, I feigned ignorance.

"I've been trying to learn more about Islam but can't seem to understand this particular verse in the Qur'an."

His eyes widened with surprise as a smile burst onto his face. "Which verse?"

No American had ever visited his house, and he never expected that an American would want to know more about his religion.

I asked, "Do you have a Qur'an?"

He smiled again. He leaned over to get a copy that was on a small table beside him.

I carefully made my way to the Verse of the Sun near the end of the Qur'an and read a few lines quietly until I got to the place I wanted to discuss. Then we sat there for ten short minutes, talking about how the Qur'an describes ancient civilizations.

My strategy worked. In graduate school, I'd written a paper about how the Qur'an and the Bible describe ancient civilizations, so I understood the passage pretty well. I just wanted to create a connection with him. I wanted to show him that Americans cared about his religion and were willing to learn from him.

He was dead.

The first time I met Galeai, I expected him to tell me the kind of thing most of the other Marines said about religious leaders: "Those are the motherfuckers preaching sermons that say 'Kill the infidel.'" But he was thoughtful. He had never considered the benefit of building relationships with religious leaders. He agreed to talk with me over the course of a few weeks and ultimately decided to give my project a chance.

He was dead.

Those were my friends at that meeting, and now they were all dead.

I couldn't stop hearing that phrase, "They're all dead."

And I was alive.

When the time came for Nicole's memorial service, Mark and I flew to Baghdad and sat in the back of the room while Iraqis and Americans stood up to talk about how amazing she was. Part of me wanted to stand up and talk about how Nicole had taken care of me during my worst times in Camp Fallujah, but I just sat there rolling a cigarette between my fingers and hoping it would be billowing smoke from my lips as soon as possible.

I had the same reaction when I went to the memorial service for the Marines. I was surrounded by my brothers and sisters—by then the Marines considered me to be part of the family—anxious to get back to the mission. An unshakable feeling was starting to grow in my belly—survivor's guilt.

It took only three months in Iraq for my world to explode. In that time, I had already been shot at in the worst parts of Iraq that dying started to feel like my destiny. Working in Iraq was a dream come true, so I started viewing death as an acceptable outcome. At no point, however, did I think it would be the destiny of the people I cared about. I was willing to die for the mission. I didn't want other people to die.

As days turned into weeks, my only comfort was recalling the conversations I'd had with Brian in Leavenworth. I finally understood the pain he choked back when I asked too many questions. Rather than face the pain of death, I convinced myself that a true hero bears the pain in silence. Success in Fallujah was my only salvation.

Mark and I pushed each other even more to make a difference in Fallujah. I went out on ever more dangerous patrols and spent more time living with Marines on bases that had no running water or kitchen facilities. I organized classes on the Qur'an and Islamic history for the Marines and went on a road show to as many patrol bases as would have me to talk about the religious leader engagement program.

I never had any way of knowing whether those trainings were useful until I was sitting in a terminal at BIAP and a group of ragtag Marines approached me and my team. We had been waiting for a flight back to Fallujah for close to twelve hours when they ran over to us. We didn't know what to expect until the leader flashed a wild grin and thrust his hand toward my chest, saying, "Hey, you're Mr. Thompson, right?"

"Yeah, who are you?"

We stood there shaking hands while he introduced his Marines. "Oh, you don't remember us? You came out to visit us a few months back. Yeah, we remember you, you were talking to us about gender roles and Islamic history…like how we needed to understand how other people saw the world, not just how we see things."

I looked at my team, confused. I was staring at a bunch of nineteen-year-old kids who were talking about gender without giggling or gyrating.

"Yeah, you know, we started to notice a lot of things about the role women play in our patrol area…some of it makes more sense now, and we just wanted to come over and thank you."

I didn't remember any of their faces, but I remembered being at their base. Their squad leader had forced them to listen to me right after they had gotten back from a long patrol, and half of the guys were sleeping or playing with their guns while I was talking. I felt like an itinerant preacher sharing what I knew about Islam with any Marine who would listen. Most of the time, I assumed that no one was paying attention, and even if they were listening, I thought they wouldn't remember anything I said.

When those Marines found me at the airport, it was the confirmation I needed.

The more I poured myself into work, the more I was able to make a difference. After a series of interviews with farmers around Fallujah, I convinced the Marines to redesign the access control points to Fallujah so that farmers could make multiple trips with their crops per day. Every farmer I talked to said the lines at the gates were so long that they could barely get one shipment of goods through in a day. They had crops that were rotting in the fields for the simple reason that the Marines had walled off their most important market, Fallujah.

Once we redesigned the access points and identified a cold storage facility near the city, we saw an increase in traffic and heard from the farmers that their revenue had grown. There was no way for us to ever know, but we hoped that their increased income would make them less inclined to take money from terrorists. One of the first things I learned about Fallujah—before I had ever set eyes on it—was how the Marines had attacked the city and built that wall. I wasn't able to tear it down, but I was responsible for helping change the burden it placed on the communities in the area.

I kept going until I was the last person from the regimental staff on Camp Fallujah. The camp was decommissioned in September 2008, and the COC had long since been relocated to al-Asad Airbase in Western al-Anbar Province when I finally left. The Marines moved to al-Asad because their mission had changed. They went from actively patrolling and hunting down terrorists to passively supporting Iraqi forces who were supposed to protect the area. It was part of the US strategy to enable Iraqis to take control of their own safety and send the Marines home to their families.

It was a sound policy, but it made it almost impossible for me to do my work since the Marines weren't in control of the patrols in the communities in which I had spent so much time. It meant that there were no Marines living out in Iraqi communities who needed my help understanding the religious terrain. Life in al-Asad was boring, and by January 2009, I started looking for a new job in the United States. When my one-year anniversary rolled around in March, I went back to Chicago to decompress with friends and interview for two jobs: as a researcher with Gallup, the polling company, and as a Persian Gulf analyst at US Central Command (CENTCOM) in Tampa, Florida.

It never dawned on me to go back to school because, by then, I was addicted to war.

Cracks in My Armor

On my first night back in Chicago, I met up with graduate school friends who had no idea I'd been to Iraq. We were sitting at the front bar of Woodlawn Tap when they started talking about how President Bush had invaded Iraq to steal oil. It had been only a year since I was steeped in the politics of the University of Chicago, but I had completely forgotten that there were people sitting on the sidelines speaking with conviction about the war. I had been so busy changing the world that I didn't fully appreciate how deeply I had changed myself to deal with the trauma of war. I was a new person—again.

And the new Alexs Thompson could only hear them disrespecting Lance Corporal Brown.

Lieutenant Colonel Galeai.

Nicole.

I drank faster to keep from yelling at them, but the faster I drank, the more my anger turned into something I could neither understand nor control. I got up and walked back to the dance floor to shake off whatever was starting to overwhelm me. As I stood against the wall, moving with the music, I tried to convince myself that I was just getting reacclimated to normal life and the beers were hitting me faster than usual. I tried to convince myself that if I could find a familiar face, I could get lost in the energy of the night. But the more I talked to myself, the more I realized that something was wrong: people who are okay don't need to tell themselves that they're okay.

I tried to focus on the bodies of awkward, drunken graduate students gyrating to the deafening rap music, but nothing seemed to work. My thoughts grew more disorganized, and I was losing perspective on the world around me.

Putting one foot in front of the other helped a little, so I headed back to the bar, but as I sat there with my friends, things only got worse. *What's going on? Wait. What did she say?* I was scrambling to focus on the conversation.

It felt like a slow drowning.

I felt like I was being dragged into a watery hole in the floor beneath me by emotions that didn't have images or sounds.

It felt like someone was standing on my chest and I couldn't get a full breath.

It felt.

All I could do was feel.

The more I struggled against the growing sense of desperation, the more I was being dragged into some dark emotional prison. The worst moments in my life had always been accompanied by a sense of speechlessness, an onslaught of emotion so powerful that my brain—my most treasured asset—couldn't save me. I had learned from a young age that it didn't matter what was going on in the real world—as long as I created a new reality in my mind, I could survive. I had spent the rest of my life learning how to implement plans to bring those imagined realities to the world around me. It meant that I was constantly reinventing myself, but it was the best way I knew how to survive.

As I sat there, staring into the mirror behind the bartender, I could only feel—there was no imagined reality that I could force into the world around me. There weren't even images of bodies twisted in death or sounds of the dying that I could resist. There was just emotion. My pain grew so intense that I didn't even know what I felt. I just felt.

The expression on my face must have revealed my struggle because my friends started asking me what was going on. I fought violently to find something in the present reality—a face or a voice that could keep me from descending into an abyss—but I failed. I struggled to force words out of my mouth, but I was caught up in a past reality that fully encompassed my consciousness. By the time I was released from that experience, my friends had ushered me back to my hotel and put me to bed.

I woke up the next morning still trying to convince myself that I was okay. It took close to twelve hours, but I started to formulate coherent thoughts about my emotions: I felt guilty to be alive.

They died for a good cause. They are the real heroes. We made a difference.

I told myself it would be a betrayal of their memory if I mourned their loss.

Would you want someone to be sad for you? Don't disrespect their memory by feeling sorry for yourself. There's nothing wrong.

I didn't know those thoughts were the first signs that war was having the same effect on me that it had on Brian. I lulled myself back to sleep with heroic stories of those I'd known in Iraq while repeating a simple phrase, "Everything is fine."

***

When I finally rolled out of bed, I wandered around Hyde Park until I screwed up the courage to see if Marvin Wilde was in his office. I knew I could never tell Marvin that I had worked in Iraq, but I needed his perspective on where my life was headed.

"Alexs, how are you? What have you been up to?"

In some ways, it felt like coming home when I walked into his office. He sat there with his back to the window and I settled into the same chair where I'd spent hours discussing anthropological theory with him.

"Well, I've been taking a little break and doing more research for my dissertation."

"Good. Are you ready to submit your dissertation proposal? I hope so. We need to keep you moving so you can graduate."

The next step of my PhD process was to turn in a paper that explained my dissertation topic and provided an overall outline. It was a formality, but I needed to declare my intention to complete my PhD after having taken my qualifying examinations. I figured I could finish my dissertation in my spare time when I got my next job.

"I'm not finished with the proposal, but I plan to submit it in the next few weeks. But…I wanted to ask you a question."

"Sure, what is it?"

"I've been interviewing to work with General Petraeus at US Central Command in Tampa."

Marvin was immediately angry. "What?! What kind of job?"

"They are looking for someone who is an expert on the Persian Gulf to help them formulate better Middle Eastern policies."

Marvin laughed. "Middle Eastern policy? What policy?"

"General Petraeus is trying to change things, Marvin. He's been advocating a policy of counterinsurgency that puts the needs of locals above our interests."

"General Petraeus? How could you think about working with him? David Petraeus represents the worst of this broken administration. If you work with him, you are a collaborator in the advancement of an evil agenda!"

For a moment, Marvin and I forgot that we were friends and stared at each other with anger that turned into surprise.

I spoke first. "Marvin, I'm trying to make a real difference here. I know our policies are screwed up, but should I just sit on the sidelines and criticize when I can actually help? You've trained me to be critical. To never back down when people rely on their fears and biases to make decisions. Don't you think I should put that to use for the common good?"

Marvin took a deep breath. "Alexs, I understand what you are feeling, but these wars are being waged by egotistical men who are hell-bent on stealing oil and destroying these countries…probably for generations to come. They don't care about local citizens, and if you believe that, you're deluded."

He could barely control his fury. We sat in silence for another moment before he continued. "Look. I respect your desire to make a difference, but you're wrong on this…I just…I can't continue to work with you if you take that kind of job."

I sat there for a moment, absorbing what he was saying. Finally, I asked the only question that mattered. "Can we still be friends?"

"...I don't know."

I walked out of Marvin's office and stumbled around the campus in a daze. Marvin had been my doktorvater and one of my best friends. It had been a risk to talk to him, but I thought that we would be able to put aside our political differences and maintain our relationship. For several long moments, I felt abandoned and alone. My shock was quickly replaced with the kind of defiant resolve I had developed when dealing with Barry. Marvin's reaction reminded me that there would always be people who resisted my unwavering commitment to the mission. Life in Egypt, Oman, Yemen, and Iraq had been the fulfillment of my wildest dreams. In another short moment, I erased the feelings that had overwhelmed me the previous night and recommitted myself to the mission. I refused to be distracted by people like Marvin who would never understand the sacrifices people were making in Iraq. I decided to work with General Petraeus.

Later that night, Tommy and I were sitting at The Pub when I got a call from SOSi, the consulting firm that would employ me for the CENTCOM job. Over the next few weeks, I began my new job orientation, found a new dissertation adviser, and had my belongings shipped from al-Asad to Tampa.

***

Within two weeks of landing in Tampa, I was standing in front of a packed room at CENTCOM, telling General Petraeus about a series of recent visits by senior Iranian officials to countries throughout the Persian Gulf. I should have been nervous, but I was exactly where I wanted to be. General Petraeus asked questions that showed he already understood the political and religious situation. "Why are Iranian diplomats traveling around the Gulf? Have you seen anything from the religious leaders in Saudi Arabia?"

"No, sir. We haven't heard anything as yet, but it's something we're monitoring. It will help us understand whether religious leaders see this as a religious move masked as a political engagement."

"That's what I was thinking. Let me know if you find anything. Thanks."

Petraeus was one of the smartest people I had met in the military because he was always curious about new ways of thinking. If I had been able to work closely with him the entire time, I probably would have lasted longer than six months at CENTCOM. Unfortunately, too many of my interactions were with generals who didn't seem to have the knowledge required to make strategic decisions for the Middle East. Far too many of them seemed more concerned with making rank than the Marines and Iraqis who were putting their lives on the line to achieve America's objectives abroad. After a few weeks, I found myself thinking more and more about Brian's experiences in the Army.

I sat in one meeting where a three-star general proclaimed that all Muslims were extremists and that there was no way we could put an end to terrorism except to kill religious zealots. Each of the people on my team took the time to explain the religious history of the Middle East, but he wouldn't believe us. We talked about intellectual movements in Iran and Egypt that challenged the importance of religion, but he was doubtful. When we talked about Arab socialism that was built on atheism, he scoffed. He was one of the senior generals in charge of our military policy in the Middle East and had no knowledge of the diversity of Middle Eastern history. No one on my team thought a senior US military leader could be so wrong. The worst part wasn't that he was uninformed, but that he had the power to impose his ideas on how we developed policy. He had long since concluded that overwhelming air power was the only way to advance US interests in the Middle East.

But I refused to give in to the culture. After a number of conversations, I got everyone on my team together and devised a plan to change cultural biases among the military leaders. We hosted weekly lunch conversations where each of us presented original research unrelated to any military operations so we could help them better understand the Middle East. In just a few short weeks, we had people from all over CENTCOM attending our lectures and seeking us out for advice. It started to feel like I was changing the world around me: we identified a topic that the military leaders were convinced they understood and presented them with evidence to challenge their ways of thinking. Our team got together multiple times a week to come up with new topics, suggest research materials, and provide supporting arguments from other parts of the Middle East.

For a while, it felt like being in a graduate school study group. We had three other experts on the team, one each for India, Pakistan, and the Levant, and I was the Persian Gulf expert. We all had graduate degrees and were committed to exposing the military to a new way of thinking. Our conversations led to writing more papers that we were able to present to General Petraeus and his staff that helped shape the future of US policy in the Middle East.

As our influence at CENTCOM grew, though, we were challenged by another civilian consultant. Layla was a young Lebanese Christian who hated Muslims. She had grown up in a suburb of Beirut and had been deeply affected by living in a Muslim community. When she finally received her American citizenship, she got a security clearance and worked her way into a position that allowed her to affect US policy. All the generals gave her the kind of one-on-one access that the rest of us wished we had. Everyone in our chain of command, from the colonel who was in charge of our team to the three-star general who reported directly to General Petraeus, opened their doors for her whenever she knocked. The rest of us had the words "busy calendar" thrust into our faces by secretaries who didn't bother to learn our names.

Layla was one of the people who convinced the senior leadership that Muslims were fundamentally violent people because it was a part of their religion. She believed that military action was the only way for us to achieve our goals in the Middle East. Most importantly, Layla was keeping me from changing the world.

It didn't take me long to confront her ideas directly and publicly. "I worked with Marines in Fallujah who barely had a high school degree who weren't as ignorant as you are. You can't dismiss all of the good people in the Middle East because they're Muslim. You can't just judge a billion people based on the actions of a deranged group of assholes. We have a responsibility to give the generals objective assessments of the situation, not bullshit prejudices."

It was one of the first times I had confronted someone so publicly and so forcefully. It felt like the world of change that my team and I were instituting was being snatched away, and I didn't know how to respond except by raising my voice. She ran out of the room crying.

The fallout was quick and unanimous:

"I agree with what you said, but you know how she is with the generals."

Or: "I'm just glad you said it and not me."

My response was always the same: "It needed to be said."

I was blind to the impact of my unwavering commitment to the mission until a few days later. One of the generals started a meeting by asking me if I was fluent in Arabic.

"I've studied Arabic for a while, but it's not my first language."

He threw one of my reports on the table.

"So how do you know your translation and analysis of these articles from Oman are correct? How do you know anything about Arabs?"

Layla was sitting next to him, glowing with excitement. She had done exactly what everyone thought she would do; she had convinced the generals to make an example of me.

I walked out of the meeting. I didn't apologize to Layla, and I didn't try to defend myself because I knew we weren't talking about Middle Eastern policy or my analysis of events in Oman; he was defending the honor of someone who shared his views. As I stormed down the hall to my desk, Marvin Wilde's voice haunted my memory:

"Middle Eastern policy? What policy?"

Although our team continued to fight for cultural change at CENT-COM, the tides had turned in favor of Layla. It was the first time I had inklings of doubt about the commitment of our leaders to the mission of bringing stability to the Middle East. We saw some success with our peers and junior officers, but it was difficult to understand how we could have the type of impact we wanted with the senior leaders. For as long as I could, I reminded myself of what Nicole had said: "We have to figure out how to ease the suffering wherever it is."

We redoubled our efforts with the people who would listen and waited for the day we could engage those who wouldn't.

In Iraq, there were two classes of people: fobbits and operators. Fobbits never went outside the wire, the safety of the base. They spent their entire deployment sitting behind a desk writing reports for people who actually went out and interacted with Iraqis. Operators spent their days and nights living in awful conditions, getting shot at, and eating meals out of a bag. Even though I was a civilian, I had been considered an operator because I spent most of my time outside the wire. I didn't even talk about getting shot at or being blown up because I was so used to it. When operators got a chance to return to bases like Camp Fallujah, they were like high school football players walking the halls in their letter jackets before a pep rally. Fobbits were the socially awkward nerds who did their home-work and secretly hated them.

I didn't realize my status until we were in a regimental meeting in Fallujah and the colonel turned to me and said, "Alexs probably has a better idea than anyone else in this room what's going on in the province because he spends so much time out in the field."

Those who didn't know me were surprised to see a civilian receive such high praise from the colonel. Those who knew me understood.

Eventually, writing reports that didn't seem to bring about change in Iraq made it hard for the operator in me to breathe—I felt like a fobbit, and it was unbearable. In Iraq, I was living the mission. Tampa became just a job.

***

By August 2009, the operator in me was convinced that I could only be happy in a combat zone. I called Brian and told him, "Things here are all sorts of wacky, brother. I'm not sure they care about what's going on in combat."

Brian laughed at me from his base in Afghanistan. "You're just realizing that? I tried to tell you that in Leavenworth, but you wouldn't listen to me."

"Well, it wasn't like that in Iraq."

He laughed again. "How naive are you? Do you really think that anyone cares about this bullshit? Just make your money and be happy."

"That doesn't help."

"I'm trying to help you. You just don't realize it."

"Then why are you laughing so hard?"

I could hear him smile. "Well, since you want to be a dumbass, do you remember Erica from Leavenworth?"

"Uh…yeah…is she the one who left a couple of months into the program?"

"Yeah, her."

"Okay, what about her?"

"Well, apparently, she left Leavenworth to go work in Afghanistan, and she's looking for people to work with her there. I'll tell her to call you."

"Okay, thanks."

Erica called the next week and told me she was managing a program in Kabul that funded Afghans who were rebuilding their society. Development Alternatives International (DAI) created vocational programs that taught carpentry, helped widows open businesses, and built government centers in communities around the country. Erica said that she was having trouble finding people willing to work in the most dangerous parts of Afghanistan.

"Most aid workers are in their mid- to late twenties and are used to living in small villages in African or Asian countries with the Peace Corps, but they're not used to dodging gunfire."

"It sounds like they want a paid vacation."

Erica laughed. "Yeah, that's how it feels sometimes, but…no offense…we don't normally hire veterans because we're worried that foreign governments will think we're trying to spread propaganda. In this case, though, there's no way we can implement all of our projects without finding people who are used to working in a war zone. We're desperate."

"I'll go. When?"

"Well, that's not my thing. Let me have someone call you in a few days, and she'll be able to tell you what the timeline is."

In a few days, Erica's regional director called me to offer the job, and I accepted. I understood the job in Afghanistan immediately: they needed people to go to the worst places and make a real difference. It was exactly what I needed to reinvigorate my spirit and recapture the hero status I had experienced in Iraq. As an aid worker in Afghanistan, I would be the money man. I'd get to design and fund my own projects, and it made me feel like I was going to have an even greater impact there than in Iraq. In the few weeks between packing my stuff up in Tampa and driving back to Chicago, I fantasized about building roads and teaching Marines how to engage religious leaders. Little did I know that I would always remember Iraq as the highlight of my career.

Within three weeks, I had resigned from SOSi, left Tampa, and was on yet another airplane descending toward a country I'd never seen before with no real idea about how I was going to get from the airport to wherever I was staying. It was that comfortable discomfort I'd come to expect.

Afghanistan

I left for Afghanistan in October 2009, and as the plane approached Kabul, I looked out the window to see a sprawling brown city nestled in a depression surrounded by the towering Hindu Kush mountains. As we got closer, the plane started making an ever-steepening, sickeningly slow descent, and I should have known immediately that Afghanistan was going to be different than Iraq. There were no screaming soldiers shuffling me off the airplane since it wasn't a military airport, and I barely recognized the civilian-clad security guards who were tasked with taking me to my new home.

As we drove through the streets of Kabul, it felt more like my years traveling through the Middle East than living on military bases in Fallujah. Even though Afghanistan is technically in Central Asia, Kabul felt like arriving in Cairo or Seeb, not rolling through the Iraqi countryside for the first time in Fallujah. There weren't convoys of Humvees or battalions of Marines running around. The streets were filled with the activities of normal life: women in various levels of covering, donkeys hauling carts, and dust everywhere. Our Toyota pickup truck was armored, but it blended in with the life unfolding in front of me.

When I was shown my room in a massive house in downtown Kabul, I wondered if there was even a war going on. DAI had rented several blocks of houses that were occupied by Brits, Aussies, Kiwis, and Americans, protected by teams of Afghans. In Fallujah, we had lived on bases that were defended by young, angry Marines who had lots of armor and bullets. In Afghanistan, I had my own room with a private shower and toilet. The houses where we lived and worked were big, with marble floors and staircases that wandered leisurely around outdoor courtyards. One of the words Marvin Wilde liked to throw around about the "occupation" of Afghanistan and Iraq was that it was *colonial*—I had never understood that when I lived on dusty bases in Iraq. Afghanistan was a different reality.

Once I put my clothes away and ate a quick lunch, I spent the rest of the day training with other DAI new hires in a large living room in a neighboring house. They taught us about how international development projects should be designed, what the military's purpose was, and the paperwork required to disburse funds to Afghans.

At the end of the day, Erica pulled me aside as I walked out of our makeshift classroom and we hugged. "How are you?" she asked me. "Thanks so much for coming; we've really been struggling to find people."

"Yeah, it's no problem. I'm looking forward to seeing how I can help."

"How was Iraq? I heard about Nicole." We had all spent time together in Leavenworth and Erica was trying to reconnect.

"Iraq was great. We did a lot of good work. How are things here?"

We both stared at each other for a moment. I could tell that Erica wanted to talk about things I wasn't ready to talk about. After an awkward silence, she replied, "It's tough. We have a lot of work to do and not enough people to do it. I hope you're ready to work."

"I sure am. Where am I going?"

"Helmand Province—Nawa District."

"When do I leave?"

"Well, we still don't have any living quarters, and we're not exactly sure how we're going to get you out there, so we'll let you know."

"Okay, just let me know when you get transportation. I can figure everything else out on my own."

"Perfect."

Erica smiled and walked away.

A 6.2-magnitude earthquake rippled through Kabul my first night there. I was being shown the town by a new coworker, Teodora. She was a Serbian from my training class who had been working in Afghanistan for the past three years and had recently joined DAI. She and I hit it off immediately, and she invited me on a tour of the bars in Kabul. I couldn't believe it until I saw it with my own eyes, but there was every kind of restaurant and bar I could ever want: Italian, Chinese, Lebanese, and a genuine British pub named The Gandamack.

We had just walked through two levels of security guards, blast walls, and a metal detector before we emerged on the vast courtyard of L'Atmosphere, one of the most popular bars in Kabul. That's when the lights began to flicker.

"L'Atmo" was supposed to be safe, but when the lights flickered and the ground started to shake, I assumed we were under attack. Before I could make a mad dash for a bunker that didn't exist, the generators kicked in, and suddenly there were no mangled bodies on the ground.

After everyone settled back into their normal drinking routine, Teodora started sharing her life story. "Have you ever seen a city on fire? Do you know what it's like to lose everything that matters to you and see everyone around you lose their everything?" She was leaning over the table, almost spilling her drink. "I know what war is like. I lived through it. I can help these people. I feel what they feel."

She wasn't talking about Afghanistan. Teodora was from Belgrade and vividly remembered NATO bombing her city to pieces. Her reaction to the pain of her own war was to help women recover from physical and mental destruction. She was on a mission to change the world, and the spark in her drunken eyes matched the spark in mine. We spent the next week training during the day and touring the city at night while we talked about how we could change the world. I knew right away that Teodora and I would be best friends. She was motivated by a passion to save the world and was willing to do whatever it took to accomplish that mission.

***

After a few weeks of training in Kabul and getting to know Teodora, I finally made it to DAI's regional headquarters in the city of Kandahar. It was geographically closer to Nawa, but Erica still hadn't figured out how I would get to Nawa or where I would sleep when I finally arrived. Kandahar felt like the Wild West. Situated southwest of Kabul in the bottom third of the country, it was considered one of the most violent provinces in Afghanistan. Kandahar had vast areas that were ruled by tribal law and bred violent fundamentalists in droves. No one was safe in Kandahar. Even the provincial governor and the chairman of the provincial council—who lived in our neighborhood—were frequent targets of assassination attempts.

In Kabul, there were still foreigners who walked back and forth to work as if it was a spring day in Chicago, but that was impossible in Kandahar. At any moment, terrorists could pop out of a bush and kill everyone in sight. I never felt safe in that massive house in downtown Kandahar, and it was a welcome relief when Erica finally let me know that I had been officially assigned to a company of Marines in Nawa District. There were no direct flights from Kandahar west to Nawa, so I had a layover at a DAI house in Lashkar Gah, the capital of Helmand Province. Once the DAI team in Lashkar Gah could get me onward travel, I'd make my way to Nawa.

Life in Lashkar Gah was similar to life in Kandahar. We lived in the middle of a normal, residential neighborhood with a predominantly Afghan security team that guarded us around the clock. The security guards were managed by a Fijian and a Brit, both of whom had been elite soldiers in their countries. We had an Afghan cook and a full staff of Afghan office workers who processed our paperwork. There was only one other development worker, Faisal, an Iraqi who had an American green card. Faisal worked full-time out of Lashkar Gah, making sure everything went smoothly and managing the relationship between DAI workers and local Afghans who applied for development grants. I sat around our house for a few days before the security lead arranged a flight from Lashkar Gah to Nawa on a V-22 Osprey with the Marines.

Nawa was primarily a Pashtun community south of Lashkar Gah that was a stronghold of the Taliban. Nawa, like many communities in Helmand, was an attractive location for the Taliban because it generated significant revenue from poppy seed production that was used to make heroin around the world. The Marines had arrived in the summer of 2008 and set up Patrol Base Jaker in the middle of the city center. They quickly reached out to political and tribal leaders to rebuild the community so that the Taliban couldn't regain control—and the one thing the Marines needed was more money. It would be my job to pay Afghan contractors to complete projects that helped Afghans resist the influence of the Taliban. My first plan was a road repair project that would connect Afghans who lived in a remote part of the district to vital services like clinics, markets, and government buildings.

I felt like I was back home. Afghanistan wasn't my home, but the pointy end of the spear was where I felt most comfortable. I was living with a company of Marines who didn't think about foreign policy or the nuances of Islamic theology; they were just trying to stay alive and make it back to their loved ones. Jaker was one-tenth the size of Fallujah, so I would be spending more time with a smaller group of people—Marines and Afghans both. Although I was hired to disburse funds, I knew that my religious and language studies would help me connect with local leaders to make a real difference. For all the differences between Iraq and Afghanistan, I was starting to feel like I could get back to doing what I did best: changing the world.

After a few days getting acquainted with the Marines, I organized my first walking patrol in Afghanistan. Every step through the farms around Nawa brought the terror of a lone Taliban sniper emerging from a poppy field to kill us. The young Marines in charge of my security seemed oblivious to the danger that lurked around us. They had stared down the enemy on the only path to the neighborhood so many times that they were just ready. I expected the Marines to be switched on at all times, fingers on the trigger, and walking slowly and deliberately with their heads on a swivel, taking in everything around them. But these Marines were experts at their job. They were observant without being paranoid. They knew they were at a disadvantage, and if they were attacked, there would be casualties. They also knew that they could react to an attack and gain the advantage quickly.

Whenever we were forced to walk single-file through a dense patch of vegetation or a washed-out road, the Marines would instantaneously take a defensive position at the sound of a broken twig or an animal running across our path. One moment we were ambling down the path, and the next moment everyone was on one knee, preparing to engage the enemy with a firearm of some sort pointing in every direction. Once the stray dog was spotted, everyone popped up and resumed their conversations as if nothing had happened.

It took us two hours to travel two miles to the neighborhood. When we finally arrived at the house of a local leader, Dawud, I hugged him and offered the traditional greeting as best I could in Farsi, a language I had studied in graduate school.

"Salām, hāl-e shumā." (Hello, how are you?)

Dawud took a startled step backward. He wasn't surprised that I'd hugged him; he was shocked that an American was speaking Farsi. I had started studying Pashto and Dari—the most popular languages in Afghanistan—but in a pinch, I could always rely on Farsi—the Iranian version of Afghan Dari.

Dawud was a stately leader who quickly laid out the importance of the project. "Some of our women have died in childbirth or lost their babies because the road was washed out and they couldn't make it to the hospital. We need this road to keep our community safe."

"We're happy to help you, sir. I've spoken with the rest of my team, and we're going to start by repairing the worst parts of the road, then go back and repave the whole thing in a second project. That way we get help to the people who need it most as quickly as possible."

"That will be fine. We are just happy you can help."

"Can you show me around your neighborhood?"

Dawud's neighborhood extended for five miles down a dirt path that was connected to the main road leading to the town market. After forty-five minutes surveying portions of the road, the Marines jumped in to ask questions about security in the neighborhood, and we took off back to Jaker.

It was my first time talking to an Afghan I was in a position to help, and it was exhilarating. I started to feel like my old self. I wasn't just mindlessly going in circles from work to the bar to my home in Tampa or from room to room in Kandahar; I was embarking on my next adventure. For days, I reveled in that sense of accomplishment and devised a plan to use the road project as a way to engage with the entire neighborhood. I hoped that my reputation would grow there and allow me to move throughout the district with projects that would squeeze out the Taliban.

I didn't expect to get any work done on that first trip. I just wanted to see the road for myself and get to know the people who lived in the community. It was a fact-finding trip that would let me fill out the paperwork and get the ball rolling toward handing over a check, which in turn would fix a road and increase the Afghans' belief in our desire to help them rebuild their community.

When I finally found a seat on a helicopter from Nawa back to Lashkar Gah two weeks later, the DAI security team that picked me up asked if I was okay the moment I hopped into the armored pickup truck.

"I'm fine; why?"

The guy across from me responded, "Well, you look like you've lost ten pounds."

"Really?"

"What do they feed you out there?" another security guy asked.

I threw my head back and laughed.

They seemed puzzled. "Is the food that bad?"

"I'm sure you guys have been in places like this. There are no showers or toilets. Every few days, I put water in a plastic bag and hang it out in the sun so I can use it to wash my body after it warms up. Our toilets are five-gallon barrels in the middle of the compound

that have doors that go up to your chest when you're sitting down...
which turns out to be the best place to have communal discussions.

"I live in a metal container whose generator is broken so I can't
sleep at night because I'm shivering in subfreezing temperatures,
and I can't sleep during the day because it's over 100 degrees. The
food is the worst. It comes in a plastic bag because we don't have
any kitchen facilities. I used to think that there was nothing worse
than MREs, but now I'd kill for one. We eat T-rats, platoon-size rations that are so disgusting I literally went hungry rather than try
to shove them down my throat."

I smiled the whole time I described my new home.

One of the security guys was a former British Special Air Service soldier and assumed I was being a prima donna. "Sounds like
camping to me, mate."

"Yeah, I guess so, if camping means that your tent butts up against
the wall that the Taliban could throw explosives over."

I was living on the edge of death in one of the worst parts of the
world, fully committed to helping people who needed it most. We
all laughed and traded knowing glances about the glory of the fight.

When we got back to the house in Lashkar Gah, I immediately
went to find the accountant so I could get my initial paperwork for
the road completed, head back to Nawa for final signatures, and
start paying the contractor. The accountant gave me an unexpected
response: "I'm sorry, sir, but we can't approve this paperwork here.
If you have a small project, we can help you out, but for this size,
you'll need to have Mr. Srini in Kandahar approve it."

"Really? Can I just have him send you an email?"

"I'm sorry, sir, but that isn't the proper procedure. You'll need to have the accountants there process your paperwork and get it signed by Mr. Srini."

I was anxious to get to work, so I rushed off to the basement where the security team had their operations center and asked, "When can I get on a bird to Kandahar?"

"Well, I'll have to radio over to one of my friends on the airbase and see what the schedule looks like, but it could be another week or so."

"Really? A whole week?"

"Yeah, mate. We can't just buy you a ticket. We've gotta coordinate with a few people, and we're not high on the priority list."

All I wanted to do was get back to Nawa as quickly as possible so I could get started on Dawud's road and identify other projects. I spent the next week completing my paperwork, designing new projects, and talking to Teodora on Skype. When I finally made it back to Kandahar, the accountants approved my initial paperwork and gave me a new stack of agreements and budgets that needed to be completed before I could disburse any money. The frustration of running paperwork back and forth between bean counters was starting to get to me when my regional director, Carter, called me on Skype. He was always direct and emotionless, but we got along fairly well.

"How are things in Nawa?"

"Slow, but good. The Marines didn't have any trouble taking me out to see the road we're repairing, so I think they'll be happy to take me out to visit sites and meet with potential contractors. Overall, I have a good feeling."

"Good," Carter continued, all business. "What other projects are you thinking about doing?"

"Well, I'm not sure yet. I was only there for a few weeks and I want to make sure I understand what other projects are being developed. The Marines are doing assessments of different parts of the district and I want to ensure the money goes where it can be most useful."

He didn't seem to be convinced by my plan. "Okay. In the meantime, let me email you the plans for fifteen projects that we implemented in Kunduz Province that you can implement in Nawa."

When I got his suggestions, I realized that most of them wouldn't work because Kunduz was nothing like Nawa. Kunduz was in the north and primarily home to Uzbeks, while Helmand was overwhelmingly Pashtun and in the southwest. I tried to explain it to him. "There's no way suppliers from Kunduz are ever going to make it to Nawa. Even if they wanted to help, they'd definitely be robbed and probably killed along the way."

"What about suppliers in Nawa?"

"There are no suppliers in Nawa. There's one contractor, and he's corrupt as shit. I'm working with him, but I need to be careful. If I give him too much at one time, he'll think he has the upper hand and he'll charge us higher rates."

Carter was beginning to remind me of the generals in Tampa. He focused more on spending money and finishing projects than on ensuring that those projects helped Afghans live better lives. I had only been in Afghanistan for a few months and I was spending most of my time negotiating with fellow aid workers, not changing the lives of Marines and Afghans.

The next time I was in Kabul welcoming new team members, Teodora noticed the change in my mood. "What's wrong, Alexs?" She always waited until we'd had a few beers before she grabbed my hand.

"It's the same old story, I guess. I'm just getting frustrated with the whole process. I don't really understand how DAI operates, and I can't tell if we're having the impact we should in Nawa. We're working on a bunch of projects, but who knows if the people really see us as their best option for a stable future."

She squeezed my hand as we sat at a table in the Lebanese restaurant. "Well, first off, don't worry about DAI's processes if they don't help you make a difference, okay?"

"Yeah. That makes sense, but I don't like having to put up with people like Carter trying to tell me what to do, and I honestly just don't have any respect for him."

"You don't need to have respect for him."

"Yeah, I guess that's true."

Teodora knew I needed a kick in the butt, and she kept pushing me to focus on the mission. "The second thing is about Nawa. You need to figure out how you can best help the people there. There is no 100 percent solution. But we have a chance to make a difference. How you feel about DAI doesn't matter; what does is whether you give the Afghans everything you can."

"Yeah, yeah, yeah. You're right."

Teodora guided me from bar to bar, night after night, reminding me to ignore the trappings of everyday life and focus on the mission. Invariably, at the end of the night we would sit uncomfortably in the back of our armored truck on the way to her house, with me wondering whether it was an accident that her hand was barely an inch away from mine. I would go back and forth about whether I should lean in and kiss her and always hesitated just long enough that she had already made her way out of the car. I always told myself that I would screw up the courage the next time, but I never did.

The more Teodora tried to encourage me about our work in Afghanistan, the worse things got. When I got back to Kandahar after my fourth trip to Nawa in January 2010, I was watching TV when the shock wave of a bomb placed outside the back wall of our building pushed me off the couch. By the time my brain realized what was happening, I was in a dead sprint for the safe room in the basement.

Once everyone made it into the safe room, we locked the thick metal door and huddled on the floor, wondering what would happen next. The room was meant to hold about ten people comfortably, along with food rations, water, and computers with dedicated Internet. It didn't feel comfortable, but we sat there talking about what we had been watching on TV when the explosion hit and what we planned to do the next day. It was a surreal rejection of the reality that surrounded us, and none of us talked about the fact that our house had just been attacked. We couldn't hear anything once the door was shut, and it was over an hour before the security team radioed down to let us know the attackers had been killed.

As we stumbled our way up the stairs, we learned that they'd used a tactic that had been successful against another development company the week before. They had thrown a rope ladder over the back wall in the hope that the first suicide bomber would take out the security guards and give the rest of the attackers a chance to rush into the house and kill everyone. Thankfully, our security team learned their lesson and was able to ward off the attackers before they made it into the house. When it was all over, we went back to watching our movie as if nothing had happened.

As I sat on the couch next to everyone, feigning nonchalance about teetering on the brink of death, I had an unexpected reaction: emotion. I didn't know which emotion I was experiencing, but it was uncomfortably close to the feelings I had whenever I thought about Nicole. In Iraq, I had been scared plenty of times, but this wasn't fear. And it wasn't indifference. For the first time, the thought of my own death disturbed me.

The operator in me refused to accept that I had turned into a wuss when I left Iraq, so I ran back to Nawa as soon as I could get a flight out of Kandahar. I needed to get back to the frontlines to keep my emotions controlled. My Marines quickly organized a patrol so I could get a few signatures from Dawud. I hoped to get back to Kandahar in less than two weeks so I could withdraw the next payment for the contractor and be back in Nawa in less than a month. I was trying to outrun a growing sense of dissatisfaction. I hoped that if I could implement just a few projects in Nawa that I would be able to reclaim the feelings of success I had had in Iraq, Yemen, Oman, and Egypt.

I knew something was wrong when Dawud greeted us hastily on the road outside his house, saying, "We need to change something, dear sir."

"Okay, what would you like to change, dear Dawud?" That short sentence meant that I would need to change the paperwork again.

"We don't want to repair the worst parts of the entire road; we want to completely repave just the first mile. Then, if we have more money, we can repair the rest of the road later."

The whole point had been to help as many people as quickly as possible. "But, sir, what about the people who live far from here and have the most trouble? Shouldn't we help everyone a little rather than a few people completely?"

Word of our arrival had traveled quickly through the neighborhood, and people were beginning to show up and surround us. The Marines grew more and more uncomfortable, but I wanted to get the contract signed so we could start helping them rebuild.

Dawud turned to the crowd and spread his hands wide. "We have met as a community and agreed that this is what we want. It is best for everyone."

I didn't believe that it was a coincidence that the portion of the road he wanted to repair was in front of his house. If we followed his plan, it would look bad: the United States was appeasing a corrupt tribal leader while the rest of his community suffered. I didn't want to do it, and I had to find a way to change his mind.

I created an excuse and pulled the interpreter, Nur, aside. "What's going on right now?"

"They want to just rebuild the first part of the road."

"I can see that, but…Nur, that doesn't make any sense. Does it look like Dawud is taking advantage of the people?"

"It doesn't seem like it."

"Well, I'm going to go talk to Dawud some more. Can you ask people what they think about this idea?"

"Sure thing. I'll be right back."

I stood there chatting with Dawud while Nur attempted to elicit honest feedback from the community members gathered around us. It was an impossible situation for everyone involved. The Afghans needed this road repaired, but the sun was getting closer and closer to the horizon, and there was no way the Marines would let us be out after dark. I couldn't afford to leave that meeting without signatures from Dawud, and there was no way he was going to sign my paperwork unless I agreed to his revised plan.

Nur returned and told me they'd had a community meeting where it was agreed that they should only repair the first mile of the road. I wasn't surprised that the locals repeated exactly what Dawud had said. Everyone stood around while I went back and forth in my mind. I knew that our only purpose was to empower Afghans to determine their own future, but these Afghans were making the wrong decision. It was the kind of predicament for which the only answer was one's gut feeling.

Finally, after I hesitated as long as I could, I decided that it would be more damaging for me to try and contravene a decision that the community had made. I mumbled to myself as Dawud signed the hastily redrafted contract. "The road is not the goal."

"Sir?"

I hadn't whispered as quietly as I thought, and Dawud wanted to know what I said.

Nur heard me, but looked at me and silently asked whether he should make something up.

I decided to be honest with Dawud and gestured to Nur to translate for me. "Dear sir, I respect your great wisdom and the will of the people of the community, but I believe the best way to repair the road would be to fix the biggest problems first. But it's not my job to tell you how to run your community. I'm not here to build roads or schools; I'm here to do whatever I can to help Afghans take control of their future and build stable communities."

"Thank you."

That was all he said. And rather unceremoniously, everyone went back to where they had come from.

I was silent the whole way back to Jaker. The clarity I felt in that moment quickly faded. I had made an uncomfortable compromise, and it immediately began to gnaw at my insides. Had I forced my solution on the community, they would have been filled with resentment. The local contractor would certainly not have given his best effort, and the entire community would have seen it as another failure by the United States. Worst of all, I would have contradicted everything I ever preached about counterinsurgency: Afghans needed to be in charge of their future whether it conformed to American values or not.

Accepting Dawud's suggestion wasn't any better. I planned to start writing a new contract to rebuild the rest of the road, but it could be months before we even got the paperwork signed, much less begin construction. The most likely outcome of my hasty decision was that Dawud would be seen as a powerful negotiator who had bested the mighty United States. Worst of all, people in his community would be no closer to having access to the financial and medical benefits they needed. As we made our way onto base and I collapsed on my bed, I fell asleep asking myself impossible questions: *What if some young mother dies on her way to the Nawa clinic in the next few months? What if Dawud was just consolidating power and eventually decided to support the Taliban against the Marines? Should it be about the road?*

***

Our house in Lashkar Gah was attacked soon thereafter.

A few days after that, one of the maids at a DAI house in northern Afghanistan made it through the first round of security before she detonated a bomb.

Hossai was gunned down in front of our Kandahar house in April 2010.

By the time I found myself back in Kabul, I finally admitted to Teodora and myself that I couldn't keep working in Afghanistan. From the moments on the plane before we touched down in Afghanistan, I knew something was different, but by the time I saw Hossai lose her life, I knew that I was different—again. Not different in a new and exciting way, like when I realized I understood fundamentalists from the inside out. There were thoughts and emotions that I couldn't process; they overwhelmed me. Something about me was wrong and I didn't know what it was.

Those emotions refused to subside. I had been devastated when Nicole died in Iraq, but it didn't take me long to recommit myself to the mission; in Afghanistan, I lingered over death. I questioned every decision I made and contemplated every danger around every corner. Those emotions made me wonder whether death was worth the mission. It would take me another five years before I found the words to express those emotions, but somehow, as I sat in my room in Kandahar in the summer of 2010, I knew it was time for me to quit running. Within a few weeks, I had found a new job back in the United States.

A week after I left Afghanistan, Teodora was caught up in a six-hour firefight at her house. It would be the worst attack against DAI, and the only reason she survived was because a security guard died on top of her.

Part Four:
A Temporary Home

Trying to Go Home

It was spring 2010 when I returned home, and the city was swollen with energy. Chicagoans were out in droves, running along Michigan Avenue and playing beach volleyball against the backdrop of a shimmering lake. Across the city, free live music and street festivals invited winter-weary city dwellers to brush off their bikes, rollerblades, and sailboats to enjoy the bright sunny days and crisp nights. I had a few weeks of vacation before I started my new job and immersed myself in a new life. I signed a one-year lease for a two-bedroom apartment in Ukrainian Village with JJ, and we did all the things Lewis and I talked about doing once we were out of Afghanistan and back home. Ola's Liquors on Damen Avenue became our local bar, and we visited so often that the bartender let us pour our beers when she went out for a smoke. We ate jerk wings at Mr. Brown's Lounge and partied with the Chicago Riot Rugby Club at Tuman's just up the road. It was a dream come true.

I did everything I could to keep my inner operator distracted with normal, everday life. I hoped that those overwhelming emotions would fade into the background, but it seemed like everywhere I went there were people who wanted to talk about war. A few of the guys on the Riot had gone to the Middle East and told stories about how brave they were, how many rounds they'd shot, and the thousands of bullets they'd managed to dodge. Even when the tears dripped into their beers, they kept telling stories about the glories of war as if it would erase their pain.

They said things like, "I'd give my right arm and left nut to get back in the shit."

They wore it as a badge of honor that they had faced down the enemy and always told the same story: "Man, it was crazy! You should have seen it. There we were, just minding our own business, patrolling the streets of some shithole town when bullets started raining down from the sky like a scene from a fucking movie…"

Or: "Fuck A-rabs, those fucking terrorists, but I'll tell you what, we kicked the shit out of them. I remember this one fucking towelhead…"

The reactions from their audience were just as predictable: slack jaws, backslapping, and distended eyeballs.

When I finally told everyone that I had been in Fallujah and Helmand, they didn't want to fill in the blanks themselves; they wanted me to describe every bloody detail. I tried telling stories about bullets and explosions, but it never felt right. I wanted to talk about COIN and how important it was that we helped Iraqis and Afghans rebuild their communities, but it seemed like the only thing that mattered to everyone was death and destruction.

People started asking me questions like: "Did you see anyone die?"

Or: "What's the worst thing that happened to you?"

They didn't seem to care if we were eating dinner or sitting at a White Sox game; they wanted me to confess my worst experiences as if they were from a Quentin Tarantino movie. They fetishized violence, and I refused to take part in it.

I hated talking about war.

I hated *thinking* about war.

I knew talking was supposed to help, but it just made me feel things I still didn't have the words to explain. I lulled myself to sleep night after night with images of Marines pumping my hand and slapping my back, thanking me for helping them solve their most difficult problems.

Far too frequently for the operator inside me, though, my emotions overwhelmed my senses, and I grew worried that I was fighting a losing battle. Thankfully, I had people who kept me from drowning. If I wasn't out with JJ, I knew I could call Liam, one of the guys from the Riot. Liam was from a big South Side Irish family, and he loved to talk. We first met at the bar after practice one day, and he launched into a story with barely an introduction.

"You wanna hear something cool?" He didn't wait for an answer. "I went to school in Winona, Minnesota, and the last two years I lived with my best friends, and when we got bored, we just walked out onto the porch with a backpack full of beer and blindfolded one of the guys. We'd spin him around and tell him to point in a direction. Wherever he pointed, that's the direction we started walking in and drinking until we ran into a bar or ran out of beer."

I didn't mean to spit my beer out at such a ridiculous story, but I couldn't help it. "Are you serious? Did you live in the middle of the city?"

"No, we lived off campus in the middle of nowhere. Sometimes we ran into a bar and sometimes we wound up sitting by the creek playing guitars and bullshitting."

"You're a little crazy, aren't you?"

"No, buddy, just living life to the max. Just having a good time."

Liam was always excited about life, and he could talk seriously about wandering around town drinking or about political theory. We hit it off immediately. Whenever I went out with Liam, I knew I could sit back and spend hours laughing at his stories from playing rugby in college or working in Ireland. Most importantly, Liam helped me develop a whole new language so I could talk about my experiences in as little detail as possible. Other people liked to talk about war, but I wanted to talk about my mission to save the world. I talked about my time living with fundamentalists and backpacking through Yemen.

I felt like it would have been dishonorable to utter Nicole's name—that people would dishonor her if all they cared about was how she died. I didn't want to tell Teodora's story, and I definitely didn't want to tell Hossai's story.

I never told my story.

I didn't have to fill in the blanks for Liam; he could read my body language and keep the conversation moving through difficult discussions. I just had to call him and he'd hop in his truck and come up to Ukrainian Village. No matter the time, our routine, whether in person or on the phone, never varied.

"Hey, buddy," he'd say, "what are you doing up so early?"

"I couldn't sleep, Liam. I tossed and turned all night."

"What's on your mind?"

"Nothing, really…just couldn't sleep."

It was always a lie.

"Well, I got to drive the train last night and wait 'til you hear what I did…"

Liam gave me exactly what I needed: a space of frenetic energy that absorbed my emotions and allowed me to reflect on my experiences in the background. I never told him, or anyone, that I didn't deserve to be breathing, that I could rattle off a list of names that deserved to be alive more than me. I didn't have to because Liam helped me create a new reality. And as I sat there with my head thrown back and my hands on my belly, I thought those emotions were losing their power over me.

***

When I wasn't running around the city with JJ and Liam celebrating my newfound freedom, I was traveling for my new job. IDS was based in Washington, D.C., but I never went to their office because the training I conducted was on bases like Fort Polk, Louisiana; Fort Irwin, California; or Hohenfels, Germany. One day I'd be partying in Chicago, and the next day I'd be on a plane to some far-off place to talk about counterinsurgency operations. Those bases were chosen because they had thousands of acres redesigned to simulate the desert environments of Iraq and Afghanistan. There was a lot of sand, not much electricity, and roaming foreigners who yelled at Americans about killing their sons in a raid. Not only did the military transform those bases to replicate an environment of war, they bused in Iraqi and Afghan Americans to populate makeshift villages and city councils so military leaders could practice how to meet with and help local Iraqis and Afghans rebuild their communities.

When I went to work, it was exactly like being in Iraq or Afghanistan. I woke up early to attend the colonel's daily briefing and traveled with various units to faraway villages where we had to convince locals that it was better for their future to cooperate with the Americans rather than support terrorists. The military bused in fake terrorists as well. They ran around at night and hid in trees during the day taking potshots at troops as they traveled in convoys from one base to another. Simulated bullets and explosions disrupted our discussions about the local economy and reminded everyone that we were preparing for war.

It felt like exactly what I needed. I got to immerse myself in training Marines and soldiers about the ideals of counterinsurgency without having to worry about actual death and destruction. I sat in meetings with high-ranking officers who were genuinely stressed out by their environments, even though they were in the middle of Louisiana or California, because the conditions were so realistic. They sought me out in what little free time they had to better understand why they were being asked to shoot fewer bullets and hand out more money. I was making a real difference in how our military leaders implemented counterinsurgency principles.

Life after Afghanistan was a perfect mash-up. By the time I started to get frustrated with the bureaucracy that plagued military operations, I'd be on a plane back to Chicago. When I started to feel guilty for spending all my time partying with friends and ignoring the mission, it was usually time to head back to a war with fake explosions and bullets.

***

In September 2010, a recruiter named William from Berico Technologies got in touch with me. He was looking for an expert in religious studies with significant experience in the Middle East to participate in high-level discussions about religious leader engagement. The job would be at a military organization called the Army Directed Studies Office (ADSO) near Washington, D.C. ADSO was an Army think tank that provided independent consideration of military policies throughout the world. The work conducted at ADSO was supposed to challenge analyses conducted by the CIA and the National Geospatial Intelligence Agency.

After looking at my resume, William knew that the best way to get my attention was to appeal to my academic side, and by the third time we talked, he had me hooked. "Hey Alexs, I've been talking with some of the people who work at ADSO, and you're going to love this. It's basically like living in a graduate seminar."

I chuckled. I knew he was a recruiter just trying to get me signed up, but he'd said exactly what I wanted to hear. "What do you mean, William?"

"Well, they have a variety of teams that are focused on different regions of the world who are given research projects by generals who don't think their staff can provide adequate answers. Obviously, you'll be spending a lot of time thinking and writing about the Middle East, but you could be called in on any project to explain how different religious practices might affect military operations around the world.

"From what I hear," he continued, "they lock themselves in a conference room for weeks at a time and wrestle with really complex ideas until they come up with a solution. How does that sound?"

"It sounds like exactly what I want to be doing with my life."

I was genuinely excited by the possibility of having an even greater impact than what I had had in Iraq.

"I thought you might say that. When can we bring you in for an interview?"

Berico flew me to D.C. for an interview, and I was hired soon thereafter. ADSO was my new dream job, and I didn't think twice about leaving my IDS job, Chicago, or my friends to start the next phase of my adventure. Within a few weeks, I packed up my belongings, said goodbye to JJ, and drove halfway across the country.

***

William was right. One week after starting my new job, I was attending a class on cultivating critical thinking skills for military policy. We spent the morning discussing ways to challenge generals to incorporate cutting-edge ideas into their planning, and our afternoons were free to read and think about what we had discussed.

Our class was held in a strip mall in Franconia, Virginia, so I spent my afternoons in cafés writing about how I could help military leaders incorporate religious understanding into their planning processes. The people in my class, my coworkers, were all smart and committed to challenging the common perceptions that hampered our ability to build effective policies. Most everyone had advanced degrees in topics like economics and history and were excited to have difficult conversations about how we could revolutionize military policy. It felt like being in an intelligence-supported graduate program, and I loved it. I wasn't deployed to the pointy end of the spear, but I was helping soldiers and Marines who didn't have time to think through policy.

It didn't take me long to convince the ADSO leadership that religious leader engagement was one of those difficult questions, and they agreed to let me coordinate a conference on how military leaders should engage with religious leaders. We held it at the Hilton in Springfield, Virginia, and drew leading scholars, policy makers, generals, and journalists.

I was on top of the world—again.

Not only was I having graduate school–level discussions about military policy at ADSO, but I was leading the way into the future of COIN by bringing my experiences to the most important people in the military.

At one point in my time at ADSO, I found myself sitting next to General Stanley McChrystal in the basement of his home in Alexandria, Virginia, while his family prepared dinner upstairs. Our team had been working on a classified project about which he had firsthand knowledge. We had tried for weeks to get him to come to our office, but he was too busy, and rather than treating our meeting like a professional chore, he invited everyone to his house to debate the future of military operations.

Stan was tough. He had spent a year in Afghanistan, and he knew every person, operation, and region of the country better than any of the rest of us who had spent years studying the region. He knew President Hamid Karzai as a friend, not as a character in a political drama like the rest of us. By the time I was sitting elbow-to-elbow with him in his basement, I was certain I had the answer to our question, and he was just as certain that I was wrong.

He rubbed his chin and leaned back on the three-person couch, asking, "What's your name again?"

"Alexs, sir."

"Well. I appreciate the work you've done, but you're completely off base. Now, I know I don't have access to classified information since I retired from the Army…"

He sat up and looked everyone in the room in the eye while he curled two fingers on each hand as if to make fun of the word *classified*.

"…but let me just make this clear to you—I know exactly what you're trying to solve, and you don't have the right answer. Have you ever been to Iraq or Afghanistan?"

"Yes, sir, I have. I was in Fallujah and Nawa."

"When?"

"In 2008 and 2010."

He turned to the rest of the team. "How about the rest of you? Anyone else been to Afghanistan?"

The rest of the ADSO crowd wasn't sure how to take Stan's rough nature, so I stepped in. "I'm the only one, sir."

"That's what I figured."

He returned his attention to me. "I know you learned a lot in Nawa. I appreciate that you were in a tough spot, but let me explain what I learned in my years implementing counterinsurgency policies…"

He went on to give us a graduate school explanation of counterinsurgency. He described relationships and networks that none of us could ever have pieced together, all of it peppered with frequent use of *fuck* and *goddamned*. When we got back to work the next week, we completely revamped our theories based on what we learned.

***

Working so closely with smart people and important generals across the world inspired me to think about finishing my PhD in the hope that I could land a teaching job at the Marine Corps University or the National Defense University. I contacted my new adviser at the University of Chicago, Sean Wrane, and started applying for university jobs. I grew ever more excited by the prospect of teaching military officers about religion while doing independent research.

In what little free time I had, I worked feverishly on my dissertation and finally sent my committee the final draft. After giving them a few weeks to read it, I scheduled a trip to Chicago so that they could suggest final changes and I could plan my graduation. Instead of fine-tuning my ideas based on the positive feedback they had been giving me for months, they took turns in that meeting to tell me that my ideas were unfounded, that I needed to go back to the drawing board and come up with a different dissertation topic. I sat in that Swift Hall meeting room for an hour, completely confused because none of them had raised these concerns after reading earlier drafts. When it was over, Sean met with me for the next ten hours to go over my 200-page dissertation page by page and explain what I did wrong.

I wanted to yell. Ask him why no one on my committee had raised any of these objections in their emails, but I couldn't. If I ever wanted to get my PhD, I had to play nice with my advisers, so I flew back to D.C., deflated. It would take me another three years, but in typical Alexs fashion, I eventually devised a plan to finish my PhD.

Fighting Fire

W hen I moved to D.C. in October 2010, I had bought a condo in Alexandria just down the street from ADSO and joined the closest volunteer fire station, Fairfax County Fire Station 5. When I wasn't busy helping reformulate our policies in the Middle East, I was at the fire station—again. Something about the camaraderie of the fire station was akin to the camaraderie I had felt with my Marines. I didn't want to go back to war and I didn't know how to finish my dissertation, so the fire station was a great way to satisfy my inner operator.

Training at Lionville had been all hands-on, but in Virginia I had to get my EMT and firefighter certifications. EMT classes ran three times a week for only three months, but fire school took up six months at four days a week for over twenty-four hours per week—all day both weekend days and at least two nights a week. When fire school started in July 2011, there were fifteen other people in my class who were crazy enough to think that running into burning buildings or breathing into cold dead bodies was a good idea. Just two weeks into the training, there were only ten of us left because the instructors hit us fast and hard. Our first module was surviving a torture chamber—"the maze."

The torture chamber consisted of getting dressed in full gear that covered our entire bodies with heavy fire-resistant material. After we donned our face mask, air pack, and gloves—all of this in blazing summer heat—the instructors pulled black cloth bags over our faces so we couldn't see. The sensory deprivation wasn't complete until the instructors put rock music on full blast and locked us one by one in an old dilapidated building on the academy grounds that had been converted into an obstacle course.

I was second in line, and they started yelling at the guy in front of me the moment his vision was snatched away: "Do a right-hand search, Sisson. Your right hand better not leave that wall!"

I could hear them yelling and banging hammers on metal trash can lids until the door shut behind him.

When he emerged almost ten minutes later, crawling out the front door, his air pack was dangling down to the side and he was pawing at the bag covering his face. Once he exposed his face to the outside world and adjusted to the light, he collapsed on the ground, unable to catch his breath. Sisson had passed his first—but not last—time through the maze.

"Your turn, Thompson!"

Instructor Gray was grinning from ear to ear.

"Yes, sir."

I ambled up to the front door, dropped to my knees, and turned on my air pack. When I heard the beep telling me the system was working properly, I put my mask on and then my gloves. When I was finished, Instructor Gray put the black sack over my face, and I connected my mask to the air pack.

"On all fours, Thompson! Let's go!"

I gingerly patted the ground in front of me, trying to remember what the outside world looked like.

"I said *let's go, Thompson!*"

I charged ahead on hands and feet, hoping I would steer myself through the front door and not knock myself unconscious.

"Right-hand search! Right hand on the wall! Don't move that right hand off the wall."

We had been training for only a week or so, but the instructors tortured us with stories of firefighters who had died because they got lost. If I put my right hand on the wall the instant I entered the maze, then I could never get lost because the worst thing that could happen was that I'd travel in a circle and find myself back at the door where I entered. At least that's what they told us.

Right-hand search. Right-hand search. Right-hand search. I repeated the phrase to myself over and over.

I heard the door shut as soon as I put my hand on the wall and turned the corner.

Then the noise started. After crawling for a moment, I felt a wall in front of me. I stopped and reminded myself what they had already taught me:

Thompson! How many sides to a box?

Four?

Is that a question?

Four.

No! There's six. Look up.

When I ran into a barrier in the maze, I slid my right hand up and down the wall to see if there was an opening above me. I didn't find anything, so I sat for another moment until I felt someone pressing their lips against my face piece, screaming, "Moooooooooooooooooooove!"

I had gotten used to the obnoxious noises the instructors were making with trash cans, but the sudden voice in my ear made me jump.

"Let's go, Thompson!"

I used my left hand to survey the path and felt a small hole in front of me that I would need to squeeze through, remembering the trick to getting through confined spaces another instructor had taught us.

You have two options. You can loosen the straps on your air pack... do not! I repeat, do not ever let go of your air pack; it's your only source of air. You can LOOSEN your straps and sling the air pack to the side and slide it ahead of you. This is the worst-case scenario. I say again! This is the worst-case scenario.

The best option is to shove your air pack into a corner and wiggle your fat body through the hole.

I took a deep breath, rolled onto my left side, wedged the air bottle into the bottom left corner of the opening, and wiggled my body through the hole.

I forgot to check for the floor when I went through the opening, and I toppled down a small decline into a pile of what felt like trash bags filled with packing peanuts.

"What are you doing, Thompson!"

Those lips were pressed against my face piece again. "You could be dead right now because you didn't check the floor on the other side of that hole."

I lay there on my back flailing around, trying to regain my bearings and find the wall, when my breathing became labored. I tried to calm myself, but it was becoming impossible to breathe. I struggled to get on my knees and find the wall when my face piece started to cling to my face—I was almost completely out of air. On our first day of class, they had worked us out in full gear until we ran out of air, so I knew I only had seconds before I would suffocate to death. I was in a full panic and started pawing at my face when someone started yelling at me:

"If you take that face piece off, you are DONE, Thompson!"

What am I supposed to do?

It took me another moment to realize the instructors had turned off my air.

Stay calm!

Pulling your face piece off was grounds for immediate dismissal because it meant you didn't have the confidence to save yourself or the firefighters in your crew. It was another thing they'd drilled into our brains that first week: *Firefighting is a life-or-death occupation. This isn't a game. If you can't keep your face piece on in training, how are you going to keep your calm when you're in a real fire?*

I slid my hand down my right side and turned the valve on my air pack until air started flowing again. I lay there, gulping in cold air until I felt those lips again: "Good job, Thompson. Now get moving!"

When I reappeared at the front door of the maze, I was huffing and puffing and pulling at my face to breathe real air. I walked over to the grass and collapsed onto my back until they called my name for another round of "fun."

The operator inside me loved the psychopathic torture I endured.

Put a 14-foot ladder on your shoulder and carry it to the top of a 35-foot ladder. Then lean over the side of that 35-foot ladder.

Tie your own Swiss seat harness out of webbing in seconds before jumping off the balcony of a three-story building.

Becoming a firefighter meant doing a lot of things I had never done before, like operating a saw and driving vehicles bigger than my Volkswagen Jetta. I attacked every impossible task with the passion I had devoted to the Middle East.

***

It helped a lot that once fire school started, the ten of us were inseparable. We went out after class and usually met up at someone's house for Sunday barbecue. Our connection didn't stop with graduation; if there was a volunteer engine to be staffed or training to be completed, we all traveled in a pack. If there was a fire department party, we all showed up together and ushered everyone to the after-party long after most people wanted to go home. They became my new family. In my first few months after fire school, I ran fires, cut people out of overturned cars, and tried to bring people back to life when their hearts stopped beating. The adrenaline of saving lives was exactly what I needed to keep my emotions from overwhelming me.

I felt so comfortable in my new environment that for the first time in my life, I started thinking about finding someone to spend my life with. My friends set me up on dates in Old Town Alexandria or fancy restaurants in D.C., but none of it excited me. The girls were pretty, but I couldn't get beyond the senseless conversations about TV shows and the latest fashions. Eventually, I wondered if I was looking for something else, so I used a pseudonym to sign up for a dating site for men. It was a sudden choice that reflected my uncertainty about where my life was headed. For a long time, I had rejected labels that were thrust on me, but I had never done anything to live out that rejection. I forbade people from referring to me as straight, Black, or male, but it barely affected how I lived my life. The point for me had always been to create the kind of freedom that allowed me to reshape myself into whoever I thought I could be.

It didn't take long before the whole process of searching for a significant other made me feel like I was reaching for something that didn't resonate with who I knew myself to be. The internal transformation that began when I moved to Chicago had been growing in the background, but I still wasn't able to focus my life on myself. So I refocused my energy on the mission. My life went into fast-forward until I truly fell in love.

Final Stop, Africa

By early 2013, I was on a plane headed to Djibouti to support a Special Forces unit that was scattered across East and Central Africa fighting terrorist groups. ADSO had been shut down by the Army due to a lack of funding, and I was hired by Praescient Analytics, another Department of Defense consulting firm. One of Praescient's chief roles was to deploy a software platform called Palantir that helped military units visualize and understand vast amounts of data about the communities in which they worked. I sat silently when they asked who wanted to work with the intelligence community in D.C. or travel the United States working with financial institutions. When they asked who wanted to travel uncharted regions of Central Africa, I uttered my favorite phrase: "I'll go."

Even though I thought I would never return to a combat zone after I left Afghanistan, I convinced myself that going to Djibouti would be a chance for me to make a difference in a completely different part of the world. I hadn't been to war in two years, and I somehow convinced myself that I needed to return to the pointy end of the spear. Characteristically, I left the fire station and all my friends to go back to war. Most importantly, I let my inner operator distract me from focusing on myself.

Praescient used what they called an insurgent model to deploy Palantir; rather than greasing the palms of powerful generals and politicians, they introduced their software to junior soldiers and Marines wherever they could. They hoped that once the junior members recognized the value of collecting their data with Palantir, they would lobby their leaders to buy more servers so that they could do their jobs better. Palantir was introduced to the military from the bottom up, rather than from the top down, the direction used by most technology firms that wanted to win million-dollar DOD contracts.

Thankfully, it was a great platform. If I had had Palantir when I was in Iraq, I would have been able to upload, code, and analyze those mosque monitoring reports in hours rather than the weeks it took me and Mark. I would also have been able to build my maps in Palantir and have one easy interface for any of the Marines to use. I knew from the moment I saw Palantir that it was going to help soldiers and Marines do their job better, and I arrived in Djibouti with the same excitement I'd had when I was in Iraq.

The soldiers I worked with immediately took to Palantir and sent me all over the continent to help those at the pointy end of the spear deploy it more effectively. Most weeks, I was being dropped off in countries I never thought I would get to visit. When I got back from my mini-deployments, I got to explore Djibouti, which had some of the best international food I'd ever tasted because it had been a French colony. There were still vestiges of fine dining scattered across the city; Luke, my coworker, and I sampled everything from French to Japanese food. Café de la Gare, on a quiet little street in downtown Djibouti, had the best steak I ever tasted, with an incredible selection of French wines. There was an Indian restaurant called Kurry run by a man named Manush whose lamb curry had me coming back at least once a week after I found his place on the outskirts of town.

When we were really looking for a good time, we went to the best hotel in town, called the Kempinski, and hit on girls. One night, we started talking to two local women who liked to hang out with foreigners, and I immediately fell in love with Maryam. It was an entirely new kind of experience. I had found myself fumbling around in the dark with other naked bodies after a night of drinking before, but I had never fallen in love. She didn't speak a word of English, so we communicated in Arabic and French; we talked about how we grew up, our dreams for the future, and getting out of Djibouti. She was exactly the kind of person I wanted to be spending my time with.

Maryam grew up in Djibouti but had opened and run a restaurant in Paris for five years before she sold it. Now she split her time between France, living the life of a socialite, and Djibouti, torturing men with her good looks. She was tall, with dark brown skin that seemed to glisten when she smiled.

I did everything I could to steal her away from the lusty eyes of every man who saw her so I could have her all to myself. I took her to the pool at the Kempinski, bought her drinks on Sunday afternoons, and splurged on Chinese food when she had a free night. For three months, Maryam was all the distraction I needed to start thinking about focusing my life's energy on myself. Until she told me she was dating someone else.

How I thought about life had changed in such a short time after meeting Maryam that I didn't know how to react. I had gone from spending my life focused on one impossible mission after another to suddenly being wrapped up in the life of another person. All the time I spent trying to date in D.C. had gone without one single person who captured my interest, and when I finally liked someone, it was ripped away from me.

Luke was the only person who knew that I was into Maryam, and he took me out to one of our favorite local bars to console me. The bar didn't have a name, at least not one that we could find, but the bartender had come to expect us once a week and made sure we got a seat at one of the four tables arranged in a semicircle around the bar. When we walked through the door, he would shout out to us, reach into his cooler full of ice, and hand us two Castel beers. Luke knew it was where I wanted to be.

"This is rough, man. You guys looked great together."

"Yeah, that's what I thought. We had a lot of fun together."

"Why did she break it off?"

"Uhh…she said she wanted to date someone else."

"I'm sorry, man…did she say who?"

"Yeah…Everett."

"Everett? Married Everett? Everett who works at HQ?"

"Yeah, that Everett."

"That's screwed up, man."

"Yeah, well, you know the worst part is he told Maryam that he's married, and apparently she doesn't care."

"That's crazy."

"Yeah. You're telling me."

As I sat there drinking my beer, it really dawned on me that I had started thinking about Maryam as someone I could spend my life with. We would have split our time between the United States, France, and Djibouti. Based on her lifestyle, I assumed she came from a rich family, and I thought I'd supplement that by doing some consulting gigs for a few months a year back in D.C. I didn't know

I was having those thoughts until I wanted to punch Everett in the face. Fantasizing about a life with Maryam felt genuine, and losing that potential was a new kind of pain.

As in every other phase of my life, I dealt with my pain by pouring myself into the mission and creating a new life without Maryam. I hadn't known how badly I wanted her when she was with me because I still didn't understand what I was searching for. So I pushed her out of my reality when she wasn't with me. I went on longer, more dangerous missions to avoid the growing feelings of unhappiness. I found myself trying to outrun my emotions once again.

A few weeks after Maryam dumped me, I was sitting on a classified base in the middle of the African continent when I got an email from Praescient saying that the company was reassigning half its employees and laying off the rest. If I wanted to keep my job, I needed to pack up my stuff and head to Bahrain. I stared at the screen for a long time. It was the middle of the night, but there were a few other guys in the cafeteria when I started talking out loud: "What in the world are you talking about!"

A petty officer turned and looked at me, but I kept talking to myself. "You've got to be kidding me. What kind of bullshit is this?"

The petty officer laughed.

"Did your girlfriend break up with you on Facebook or something?"

I shook my head. "I wish. My company just sent me an email saying that they've reassigned me to Bahrain."

"Bahrain? What's Bahrain?"

"It's a country that might as well be on the other side of the world, that's what it is."

"Why are they sending you there?"

"I have no idea."

I felt lucky to still have a job, but it was the first time in my life that there was hesitation when I said, "I'll go."

I rushed back to Djibouti and caught the next flight back to Virginia. I spent three weeks with friends and riding fire trucks while Praescient filed for my work visa to Bahrain. Not long thereafter, I was on another airplane to an unknown country.

***

Three months later, I slipped into a deep depression. I should have been happy in Bahrain. I was back working with Marines who were genuinely curious about making a real difference and were excited to have me join their team. We quickly became friends and went out to eat and have drinks most nights of the week. I played rugby, had parties in my rooftop pool, and traveled to Serbia to visit Teodora.

But something was terribly wrong, and I couldn't explain it away anymore.

It had started as an overwhelming sea of feelings in the Woodlawn Tap when I got back from Iraq, but I had been able to ignore it by focusing on new types of adventures. I don't know what finally broke my resistance—whether it was Maryam or seeing Teodora—but I lost all ability to compartmentalize the trauma of my life.

I started to wonder whether life was worth living—again.

I was still able to drag myself out of bed to go to work, but I rushed home afterward and locked myself in my apartment, turned off the lights, and sat in silence for hours at a time trying to understand what was happening to me. I yelled at myself night after night for weeks.

You're being ridiculous! Everything is fine. This is ridiculous. You're helping the Marines.

I couldn't stop myself from re-experiencing the basement in Norristown or the day Mark sat me down at the smoke pit.

Or the day I saw Hossai collapse on the sidewalk.

Or the dead bodies I'd seen in combat or as a firefighter.

I didn't have any words to express the darkness that had overwhelmed my reality—it was just one moment after another of reliving a traumatic past. As my mind spiraled out of control, I began to wonder whether anything I had done since 9/11 had been worth the trouble: I hadn't fixed US–Middle Eastern policy.

I still didn't know that I was broken inside.

I was too embarrassed to talk with anyone and ignored calls from my friends. Slowly, very slowly, a voice started to emerge in the midst of the confusion and uttered a simple phrase, *Go home.*

In a firestorm of emotions, it was a calming voice that redirected my energy.

A month earlier, Praescient had asked if I wanted to extend my assignment in Bahrain from six months to a year, and I said yes. I finally realized that was a mistake. I didn't know if Praescient would keep me employed when I returned, but I knew it was time for me to go home. Six months after I arrived in Bahrain, I packed up my things and left the Middle East for the last time.

Part Five:
A Love Story

An Introduction to Love

When I got back to D.C. in the spring of 2014, I devised a plan to fix myself. I made three promises to myself:

I'm never going back to the Middle East.

I'm going to settle down.

I'm going to finish my PhD.

They were the kind of absolutes that had motivated me all my life, and I believed I could do anything I put my mind to. I wasn't exactly sure what "settle down" meant, but it felt right. My new mission was to stay put and live out the one scene that had embodied my greatest hope when I was deployed: sitting on my front patio with friends, listening to music, and drinking cheap bear. I didn't want to be in some fancy hotel or a faraway outpost anymore. For the first time in my life, I wanted to find a boring 9-to-5 job.

While Praescient looked for a new assignment for me in the D.C. area, I turned my attention to finishing my dissertation. When I had met with my committee a few years earlier, I thought of it as an intellectual exercise to come to a shared understanding of the truth.

When I got back from Bahrain, I saw it as a war and my professors as the enemy. I spent hours every day editing the dissertation I had submitted in 2011. When they responded with vague comments, I pushed them for specific suggestions and recommendations for other books I could read to address their concerns. They ignored my emails at critical junctures and contradicted themselves when it was convenient for them. To combat their tactics, I didn't give them what they wanted. Instead, I flew to Chicago every other week and paid people on campus to let me know when they walked into their offices so I could call and pressure them to sign my graduation paperwork. I was playing dirty.

The worst conversation I had was with Dennis Marshall, the professor who had arranged for me to study in Oman and who was a member of my dissertation committee. One of my friends on campus spotted him walking into Pick Hall and called me. I hung up immediately and called his office.

"Hello, Professor Marshall, how are you?"

"I'm good. Who is this?"

"This is Alexs Thompson. How is your spring quarter going?"

"Oh…it's fine…"

I knew I had to keep him talking so he wouldn't have time to come up with an excuse to get off the phone. "I was wondering if you've had a chance to take a look at the draft I sent you."

"Well, I did, but there were some things that didn't make sense. I don't understand why you're using postmodern literary criticism—narratology—to analyze a medieval Islamic historical text."

"I understand that, Professor Marshall, but it's very similar to what Boaz Shoshan did. I just took his theories and expanded on them."

We went back and forth for about thirty minutes, with him raising specific objections and me explaining the source of my theories. Finally, in a moment of exasperation, he revealed his hand. "Look, Alexs, it's clear that you've done a lot of research and work on this dissertation. I just don't like it."

I was shocked that he had come clean. I had a suspicion that my professors were giving me a hard time because I was using modern ideas to translate canonical historical texts. He finally admitted that it wasn't just that he disagreed with me and wanted to make sure I had a strong argument for others who might disagree with me. He was stonewalling me because he didn't like the fact that I was challenging his theories. It was the proof I needed to ramp up the attack on my committee.

"I understand where you're coming from, Dennis, but I think it's important that we have fresh ideas in the academy. I've read everything that's out there on this topic, and I'm presenting my perspective because I think it will help us better understand early Islamic history. Do you have anything else I can read that might help explain my theories better?"

I was furious, but I knew that I had to play along for my plan to work.

"Umm…I'll look into it…okay, Alexs, I've got to go now, but I'll think about it."

If I had just followed the suggestions of my committee and done as I was told, I probably would have already earned my degree, but I insisted on doing things my own way. I had always done things my own way—no matter how painful it was. I refused to back down, and it made my professors angry. Even though I had listened to that voice in Bahrain that told me to go home, I was still attacking every aspect of my life as if I was fulfilling my most important life mission.

When I was satisfied that I'd made enough concessions to my committee, I went to one professor and told him that the other two had already approved my dissertation and that I was just waiting on his signature. I did that until I had three approvals on my dissertation.

It worked.

I won the war.

Once my graduation paperwork was submitted and approved, I got an unexpected email from the Dissertation Publishing Office asking if I wanted to add a dedication to my dissertation. I replied immediately and told them no. I was so fed up with the entire graduate school process that I just wanted to be finished.

When I lay down to sleep that night, however, one name kept running through my head, and after a few hours of fitful sleep, the words for a dedication started pouring out of me:

This dissertation is dedicated to Nicole Suveges. She was savagely hunted down and murdered on the streets of Baghdad in 2008. In the midst of her own PhD studies, she looked at an intractable situation and decided to act. She decided to apply the life of the mind to an impossible situation. For her insightful engagements and effective suggestions, she was specifically targeted and killed. At a time when many academics were blinded by the temptation of inaction, she chose to act. She paid the ultimate sacrifice.

I will always remember her memorial service: male, Shi'i, Iraqi clerics defied their own cultural conventions and the intended order of the service and stood up, one by one, to praise this non-Muslim, female, American scholar. They spoke about her as they would an old friend and lamented the state of the world where Nicole was moved in the deepest part of her being to separate herself from her family and offer aid to complete strangers. Yes, language is about power, but there are always people who decide to act.

I was inspired by Nicole's energy and her commitment; like many survivors, I often wonder, "Why not me?"

I sat at my dining room table in the pitch dark, furiously tap, tap, tapping away at the keyboard on my computer. The sensation of banging my fingers against the keys helped ease my emotional pain.

I didn't mean to be writing about Nicole.

I hadn't meant to use the word *survivor*.

It was the first time that I was consciously processing the last thirteen years of my life. When I finished typing, my fingers roamed around the keyboard searching for another word to type, but there was nothing else to say.

***

I graduated in August 2014 with Liam, and my dad in the audience. As we walked from Rockefeller Chapel to the private graduation for the Divinity School, I felt a tap on my shoulder.

"Hey, Mr. Thompson."

It was John Halse, the dean of the Divinity School; I had taken a class with him in my first year and we'd stayed in touch.

"Hey, Dean, how are you?"

"I'm good. You know, I always like to look at what people wear to their graduation—it tells the story of how they feel about their experience."

"Oh, yeah?"

"Yes, most people get dressed up, but I noticed that there were only three people wearing sandals this time, and you were one of them. I take it the last few years haven't gone well."

While he laughed at my flouting the unwritten rules of graduation attire, I unzipped my robe and showed him my shorts and tattered T-shirt. Then I pulled out my phone and showed him pictures of me in my robe in compromising positions at the bar, on CTA buses and subways, draped over my buddies, and wrapped around strangers who were willing to oblige an intoxicated graduate student.

I spent graduation night with friends in Ukrainian Village, and by the time I flew back to D.C., I was preparing for another chapter of my new life. With my PhD in hand, I landed a job at the Federal Emergency Management Agency as a data scientist—a job that would never send me to the Middle East. I was most of the way to fulfilling my commitments to myself, but I knew it was time for me to find someone to spend my life with. I didn't know how to accomplish that goal or why it mattered. I just knew that it needed to be a part of my plan to settle down.

I wasn't just looking for someone else, I was looking for a way to be my true self.

I'm dating.

I had to remind myself repeatedly that I was committed to finding that special someone who could share my kind of life with me.

It sounded fake when I said it, but it had to be true. It was the only thing I was missing. I'd reached for and achieved every other dream I'd ever dreamt.

I forced myself to sign up for dating sites, and it didn't take me long to run into the same problem as before: it was thoroughly uninteresting to me.

I'm dating.

I was going on enough dates to know that I was doing something wrong, so I widened my search outside the D.C. area.

I was *online* dating.

It took a few months, but by the spring of 2015, I was madly in love.

His name was Jeremy, and he had just separated from his wife after twelve years of marriage and had two little girls he adored. I found him online, but by the end of that first day, we were talking on Skype almost nonstop.

I was turned on from the first moment I saw him. Reddish tints to his beard, shorter than me, stocky, a little bit of a country accent. He loved to laugh and show off his body.

I giggled.

I don't think I had ever giggled. I was a grown man giggling with another grown man.

We were completely different people, but we were in the same boat—struggling our way through a successful life. He had everything he'd thought he would ever want, but was unhappy for some reason he couldn't completely explain. He grew up in a small town in northern Missouri where boys married girls, and he felt different. Not so different that he ran away from every social convention and reinvented himself every few years, but different enough that he had grown used to a gnawing sense of unhappiness. Everything about his life made sense: four-wheeling, back-road driving, shooting guns, smashing mailboxes in the middle of the night, partying in corn fields, and close-knit families living on farms with kids playing in the front yard were all he had wanted out of life.

There were only eleven people in his high school class, and when he was promoted to manager at the local hog farm, he planned to retire there after studying agriculture and business at Missouri Western State University. A year after he finished college, though, he received a job offer from the local bank and decided to take a chance at a new career. By the time we met, he had been recruited by one of the best banks in Kansas City and was being groomed to be a senior executive. He had come from nothing and turned his life into something he never could have imagined.

We started our relationship the way I started every friendship I'd ever had—there was an immediate connection built on a passion for living life to the fullest. We found ourselves talking about our deepest fears and greatest hopes within hours of meeting. The conversations flowed so easily that I forgot he was hundreds of miles away, living the kind of settled life that I still didn't know how to understand.

I had to constantly remind myself that I wasn't just making a new friend; I was looking for that kind of someone who could be a lifelong partner. I tried to fantasize about what it would mean to live in the same place for longer than a few months, but in those early days it was too overwhelming.

I'm dating.

I repeated those words over and over.

***

It only took a week before we said it. We were having our fifth conversation of the day, and Jeremy could barely look me in the eye.

"I know we don't know each other at all…but…I don't know, man…"

I immediately knew what he wanted to say—and I knew I felt it too. I let him stumble his way around his words. "I don't know what the fuck you're doing to me…I feel…"

"Me? I'm a world-traveling fireman and all I can do is think about you all the time."

It took us thirty minutes of pretending before we said it: "I love you."

This time, it was different than when Bret, Brian, or other people told me they loved me. I didn't know, back then, that people were uncomfortable saying those three words. It was never difficult for me because it didn't mean the same thing. "I love you" was an expression of an idealized reality—it meant that I would do everything in my power to push you to become the hero you were destined to become. Love was an expression of faith and commitment, not lust.

With Jeremy, things were different. I was in a relationship. We talked nonstop every day on Skype, through text, and on the phone. We woke up in the middle of the night and wrote each other love notes about how lucky we were to find each other. I waited for him to text me "good morning" before I started my commute, and as soon as I left work, I dialed his number and prayed he wasn't stuck in a meeting. If I missed him before I got on the train, it was an insufferable twenty minutes before I got a signal again. I was a forty-year-old man with a high school–style crush, and it felt amazing and uncomfortable. Nothing in my life had prepared me for an experience with my own emotional happiness.

Jeremy wasn't an experiment with how to solve a riddle or complete a mission; he was a new kind of opportunity to be my true self. I had spent so much of my life's energy experimenting with the most dangerous, adrenaline-fueled adventures that I had succeeded at ignoring the truth of my own everyday reality. I experimented with gender roles in Egypt, relationships in Yemen, social networks in Fallujah, economic assistance in Nawa, and burning buildings in Virginia—but I had never experimented with my own happiness divorced from some existential mission.

Something clicked when I started sharing my life with Jeremy. It was deeply uncomfortable, but the more I poured my heart into him, the more I found the courage to say the things I didn't know had been stuck in my heart forever.

"I don't know what's wrong with me," I told him one day. "Lately, it's just felt like something is wrong. I have everything that is supposed to matter: money, a condo, a great job; I've traveled the world, I have a PhD…but I feel like something is missing, you know what I mean?"

"Uhh…sure…but how much money? Like sugar daddy money?"

We both laughed.

The thing that surprised me most was how much fun we had. Talking with Jeremy felt like talking to Liam or JJ. I had always thought that a relationship would be boring, that I'd have to give up my hobbies and stop spending time with my friends. My life was defined by adrenaline, and I was afraid of being tied down. But Jeremy loved the fact that I got my adrenaline fix by being a fireman. One day, he kept asking questions.

"…but where's your fire gear?"

"What do you mean? It's at the station."

"When are you going to bring it home?"

"Uh…I just keep it at the station. Why?"

"When are you going to bring it home *for me*?"

We both laughed.

I was oblivious to love. I had loved plenty of people in my life, but things with Jeremy were different. I could feel love, but I still didn't know what it meant for Alexs to be in love. I knew that seeing Jeremy on Skype made me want to jump out of my skin. He had a hairy chest, blond hair, and deep blue eyes that convinced me to do whatever he wanted. Our connection was so real that we had little trouble expressing our feelings.

The biggest difference between us was that he had a great relationship with his family. Actually, he was better at relationships than me in general, and it always surprised me when he anticipated my emotional needs. One day, I came home from work frustrated, and he knew it before I took the time to tell him.

"I love you, Alexs."

"I love you too, Jeremy."

"Alexs?"

"Yeah."

"I love you."

"…I love you too, Jeremy."

I didn't know what was happening or why he kept asking me questions.

"Can you hear me?"

"Yeah, why, is Skype messed up again?"

"It's not Skype. I want you to feel what I'm saying: I love you."

It took my breath away. It made me feel something I didn't know how to explain.

I was in love.

I was so used to relying on my own energy. I was always so prepared for some person or job to be snatched away from me that I had never fully shared myself with anyone. I felt so addicted to whatever we had that I was ready for the next step.

"Let's meet."

I blurted it out one day barely two months after we met. I shouldn't have been afraid of his reaction since we had already professed our love for each other, but I knew that meeting had the potential to ruin our new relationship. What if the camera had hidden all of his imperfections or he was actually still married? Anyone can love anyone from hundreds of miles away, but what I said was going to change everything.

"Okay."

That's all he said. He didn't hesitate and he didn't jump for joy. He just agreed.

***

Everything about our hasty relationship felt like a fairy tale, but I was scared breathless when I drove down a long gravel road in central Missouri to meet Jeremy for the first time. It was an isolated log cabin in the middle of nowhere with dirt trails that disappeared into mini-forests. There was a big barn on the property and a short dock with a boat that led onto a lake shaded by newly budding trees. I was the first one there, so I sat on the pier for a moment, wondering whether this was where my life was going to end. I hadn't told anyone where I was going, and if Jeremy turned out to be a racist murderer, no one would ever find my body. I wondered if it was worth it. We had talked about meeting at a bar for a few beers to decide if we felt a physical connection, but by the time we agreed to meet, it didn't feel necessary. I was starting to regret that decision.

Eventually, I heard a truck pulling up the dirt road. It was Jeremy. I wanted to turn around and go back to D.C., but I pasted a big smile on my face and put one foot in front of the other. I was afraid and excited. I didn't realize until that moment that I had pinned my future on what was about to happen.

I was dressed up in a new pair of jeans with brown leather shoes and a button-down shirt. I had sculpted my beard into a handlebar mustache and shaved my head. When Jeremy jumped out of his truck, he was wearing sandals, shorts, and a T-shirt. He looked down at the ground while he shut the door and then turned to me and said, "Hey, man, how's it going?"

"I'm good."

We both moved with purpose and stuck our hands out for a hearty handshake and a manly hug.

We didn't know how to be in love.

"I brought some stuff. You want to help me get it out of the truck?"

"Uhh…yeah, what'd you bring?"

"I brought some steaks, vegetables, chicken, ice…"

"Beer?"

We both laughed and really looked at each other for the first time. Then we started grabbing bags and fishing poles.

"Have you ever gone fishing?" he asked.

"No…you wanna show me how it's done?"

"Yeah, I saw pictures of the lake, so I got two fishing poles."

His hands were shaking so bad he couldn't string the fishing poles, and it made me feel better that he was as nervous as I was. We spent the next hour pretending to fish and talking about the weather while we calmed our nerves. We were sitting on the front porch after fishing, drinking beers as fast as our bellies would let us when he changed the subject.

"Man. When I drove up and saw you coming from behind that cabin, I 'bout near crashed my truck."

He still wasn't looking at me, but he was giggling.

"What do you mean?"

He laughed, took a swig of beer, and laughed some more. "I swear. The sun was just right…" He kept drinking and laughing, trying to say words that didn't want to come out. "It was right behind you and you came around that corner and you had that big ole grin on your face…"

We stared at each other for a moment before we hopped up to start preparing dinner. He grabbed the bag of charcoal and started building a fire while I cut up the vegetables and caught my breath. Everything was quiet around us. There weren't any other houses or people for miles, and we were both left alone with our thoughts as we prepped dinner together for the first time. Things felt off all through dinner. We were acting like buddies who'd gotten away from their families for the weekend, not like two people who were in love.

Once we had finished dinner and cleaned up, we sat back down on the porch and guzzled down our beers. Finally, I couldn't take it anymore. I pushed the fear out of my head and I leaned in.

And then we kissed.

It was more like a peck. A trial run of sorts that let me see if this could be the kind of excitement I had been searching for.

The effect was immediate. I sat back down in my chair and fumbled to open my beer can. When I finally screwed up the courage to look back at him, he broke the silence. "You wanna go inside?"

"Sure. You wanna watch TV or something?"

"Not really."

***

Our weekend at the cabin convinced us that we had something worth pursuing, and things moved fast, probably too fast. We started flying back and forth to see each other when Jeremy didn't have his kids for the weekend. We didn't know everything about what it all meant, but we were committed to finding out. Our conversations grew more serious as we tried to figure out what the next step was.

"I don't want to go to gay bars and have sex with a different guy every night of the week. I want someone who will be my partner and will want to help raise my kids with me. Someone I can be proud of when we're out in public, not someone who's just looking for a good time."

Jeremy caught me off guard with how much he had thought about what it meant to find a partner. I knew I was in love, but I didn't have any experiences to help me understand how to keep moving forward.

"I never thought about it like that, Jeremy."

"Well, this is the stuff I guess we gotta figure out. What do you think?"

"I mean…I agree I'm not looking for some one-night stand. If I just wanted to get laid, I could do that, because—trust me—I got moves…"

We both laughed.

"…but I've been everywhere I ever wanted to be. Hell, I've been to places I never thought I would be. I've lived every dream. I'm looking for a new adventure, not a fling…and I guess that means settling down with someone."

I never wondered if what we had was real, but I couldn't figure out where it was going. The faster we moved, the more questions we had to answer.

"What are we doing, Jeremy?"

"What do you mean?"

"I mean, where are we going with this?"

"I'm not sure," he admitted.

"Well…I'm all in…do you feel the same?"

"Yeah, I'm committed to this thing…"

"So, what do we do next? I mean…long-distance relationships are stupid."

"…Yeah…"

"You're not saying much."

"I don't know what to say, Alexs. What we have is amazing, but… little girls need their daddies…"

"What does that mean?"

"It means I can't leave Missouri. My ex would never let me take my kids, and that'd mean I'd never see them. Or my family…I just…I can't…do that."

We stared at each other for a long moment on the computer screen before I told him I should probably get to bed.

I laid awake most of the night. I knew that Jeremy was what I was looking for. It didn't just feel good to be around him; it was starting to feel necessary, as if I had finally found a missing part of my soul that I couldn't let go of. At the same time, I knew he was right: little girls and boys need their dads.

I called him early the next morning. "You know, there's something about me I haven't told you yet, and I spent all night thinking about it."

"What is it?"

"I grew up without my dad. My dad abandoned us when I was three, and I didn't see him again until I was in college."

"I'm sorry, I didn't know."

"I know. For some reason, I didn't tell you. To be honest, it's not something I think about very much. It was awful as a kid, but we reconnected and now we're best friends. I don't know where I would be if he wasn't in my life…actually, I do know. I wouldn't be the person I am without the support he's given me.

"I've been thinking about you and your daughters, and I didn't say this last night and I should have: I would never want to separate you from your girls. I'm not asking you to move to D.C…I could never do that.

"If we want to make this work—if we're serious about each other—then I have a big decision to make."

"I don't want you to have to move for me…that doesn't seem fair."

"That's what I thought about all night. I wouldn't be moving for you. This isn't about you. It's about me. It's about whether I believe that what we have together is the thing I've been reaching for all this time…the reason that all my other accomplishments don't seem to be enough right now. If I do it, then I'm doing this for me. I'm doing this for the me I want to be."

"Does that mean you're moving out here?"

"I'm not sure yet…"

It took me a few weeks, but I was finally ready to admit that Jeremy was my future. I still didn't know what it all meant, though. The adrenaline addiction I had developed was only slowly receding. There was a blurry image in my mind of another new Alexs out there somewhere that my gut told me existed but who I didn't fully understand yet. The only way for me to find out would be to jump into the unknown. Love would be my next adventure.

When I made my decision, I started telling the people who mattered to me. I called my dad first and told him, "I found someone."

"That's great, Alexs, who is it?"

"His name is Jeremy and he's from Missouri. We've been spending more and more time together, and I think I'm ready."

"I'm so happy for you, Alexs. You really deserve this. I know you've struggled with finding someone. Tell me about him."

I told George and Kevin from fire school next. I went out to dinner with them separately, but they had the same reaction when I tried to ease into the discussion.

"You're not dying or something, are you?"

"Uh…no, but I found someone I want to be with, and his name is Jeremy…"

Kevin's fork hovered in the air for a moment as he looked at me.

"…and he lives in Missouri."

Kevin looked at me as if he thought I was joking, but when I stared back at him, he knew I was telling the truth.

"I mean," George said, fumbling for words, "I guess you've always said you don't believe in being straight or Black or whatever, but…"

Both of them pushed their food in a few circles around the plate while they processed it. I broke the silence by asking them if they were okay.

"Yeah, it's just weird. Are you moving to Missouri or something?"

"I think so. I don't know when, but I think I might be moving out there to be with him."

"That sucks, man. I mean…I'm happy you found someone…but I can't believe you're moving."

My truck lieutenant, Harry, was more blunt. "Yeah, right, you're screwing with me, Alexs."

"Nah…I'm not, Harry. I'm probably going to be moving in the next few months or whenever I find a job out there."

"No kidding?"

"No kidding."

"Well, I'm happy for you, man, and if anyone at the station gives you a hard time, just let me know and I'll fuck 'em up."

I wasn't getting the reactions I had expected. Everyone was surprised but supportive.

Jeremy wasn't ready to tell anyone because he was scared for his daughters. He was petrified that some homophobic Missouri judge would forbid him from seeing his girls. He worried about how his two young kids would deal with the news.

"What if they get bullied because their dad is gay? What if they don't get invited to any sleepovers because the parents think I'm some kind of pervert? What if my girls stop loving me?"

None of those things had occurred to me, and it broke my heart. When he finally screwed up the courage, he came out to his closest friend.

"Well, I told Lisa today."

"Really! How'd it go?"

"We worked out in the morning and when we got back to her place, we were in the kitchen making breakfast and I just started crying. I don't know what happened, but as soon as I thought about telling her, the tears just started flowing. I don't know what was wrong with me. She got scared and turned to me and said, 'Are you okay? You're not sick or something, are you?'

"I walked into the living room and she followed me because she'd never seen me cry before. She kept asking, 'What's wrong?' I finally just blurted it out: 'I'm gay and I met someone.' She got a surprised look on her face, but her words spoke her true feelings. 'I don't give a shit. I love you, and everything will be fine. Now, tell me about your man.'"

Jeremy had known Lisa since he was three years old, and they'd gone to school together from kindergarten through college. Having her acceptance meant that he could begin the process of telling people from his small town that he wanted to be with a man. Every time he thought he would be disowned by his parents or his childhood friends, they just embraced him and asked if he was happy.

There was only one bad experience, and Jeremy told me about it over Skype on his way home from work.

"I went to see a therapist over lunch today."

I had been sitting on my patio waiting for him to finish his workday. "You what? Why didn't you tell me you were going to see a shrink?"

"I don't know…I just…I wasn't sure how it was going to go, and I didn't want you to think I was getting cold feet."

"No, not at all; I think it's a great idea…we're both going through a big transition. I've been thinking about doing the same…. What'd he say?"

"It was a woman…"

"What did she say?"

"Well, I'm not really sure what to think…"

"You okay?"

He got quiet.

"Jeremy, what did she say?"

"Well, it was weird; she started asking me if I've ever looked at pornography and…I dunno…"

"Really? Are you serious?"

"Yeah."

"What else did she say?"

"I dunno…it just felt…off. Something about the whole conversation just didn't feel right."

"Jeremy, what else did she say?"

"Well…she talked about how God made men to be with women and that if I was committed to not looking at porn then she could probably help me through this. She said it would probably take a couple of months, but if I did everything she told me to do…"

Jeremy went silent for a moment.

"Okay," I said. "Let's just stop right here and get something straight. She's 100 percent wrong. You know that, right? Jeremy, look at me. What she said to you was wrong."

I was so angry I jumped up and started pacing around my patio.

"She said if I just make better choices…" Jeremy's voice faltered.

"No, Jeremy. You can't let some idiot shake your confidence or tell you who you are. We've spent our lives doing what we thought we were supposed to be doing, but this is our time. We don't know who we're going to be yet. We don't know exactly where this relationship is going, but one thing is for sure: we're headed in the right direction. Going backward is not an option. Don't do this for me; do this for you."

I could see Jeremy shaking off the shock, but he continued. "She asked me if I believed in God."

"What?"

"Yeah."

"I can't believe she would say that…well, I guess you do live in the Bible Belt. Who knows, maybe prayer does change things."

We both laughed.

***

Jeremy flew out to meet my friends, and they loved him immediately. All of my buddies from the fire department and the people I had kept in touch with from Berico and Praescient showed up to meet the new love of my life. It was the first time Jeremy got to see me in my element, and he couldn't stop talking over breakfast the next morning. "I had so much fun last night. You've got some great friends."

"Good. I'm glad you had a good time. Did you actually get to talk to anyone, or was it too loud?"

"No. That's what surprised me the most. People kept coming up to me and asking if they could talk to me. I sat with George and Kevin for, I dunno, fifteen minutes or so, drinking beer and telling them stories about growing up in a small town. They told me you're their big brother and have helped them so much. Then, what's your friend's name, you worked with him down the street…"

"William?"

"Yeah. William told me about how you guys got to be such good friends. You have some good friends, Alexs."

"I'm really lucky."

We were at the IHOP around the corner from my condo eating pancakes as quickly as they were brought to our table.

Jeremy was caught up in our new reality. "It just felt so natural. No one cared when we kissed or held hands. They just accepted us for who we are."

"What? Were you kissing me in public?"

We both laughed.

"Just once or twice," he said, grinning. "But…things are a lot different here than in Missouri, that's for sure."

"What do you mean?"

"I can't imagine doing that in Kansas City."

We were starting to find our normal. We didn't want to fit into a new culture or redefine everything about our lives. We were learning how to bring our love to the lives we were already living. It meant that our most powerful experiences revolved around cuddling on the couch watching bad movies or sitting at some bar rooting the Royals for a World Series win. For the first time in my life, normal felt good. There was a passion that consumed my consciousness, but there was also a stability that was comforting. I no longer felt like I was reaching for something; I was just holding on to Jeremy.

It seemed like everything that had happened in our lives was meant to bring us together. Just as I started my job search in Kansas City, I met up with my second team leader from Iraq in a bar in downtown

D.C. He told me that he was working for the State Department and they were sending him to Bolivia.

"That's great. I'll have to come visit you." It sounded like yet another country I could add to my passport.

"I'll let you know what it's like."

"Where's the wife and kids?"

"They're in Kansas City packing up our stuff."

I was immediately surprised. "Why are they in Kansas City?"

"Well, we bought a house there. We wanted to have an actual house to come back to when we're on vacation, and it's close enough to her parents that they can check up on it while we're gone."

"That's funny…"

He raised his eyebrows. "What? Why?"

"I'm probably moving to Kansas City in the next few months. When are you leaving for Bolivia?"

"What? Why are you moving to Kansas City?"

"Well…believe it or not, I fell in love with a dude and he's in Kansas City."

"That's not something I ever thought I'd hear you say…love."

He laughed. There were always people in my life who instinctively knew that the only thing that motivated my decisions was commitment to the mission. He was less surprised by the fact that I was with a man than that I had decided to settle down.

"I'm as surprised as you are, but things are going great, and I just started interviewing for a couple of jobs that look promising."

"You must be in love if you're thinking of moving from D.C. to Kansas City."

"Haha…good point."

"Let me talk to my wife. Our house is gonna be empty for two years—maybe you can stay there."

***

My job search went as smoothly as my new relationship. I interviewed for two jobs, and after a series of interviews, I decided to take a job as a data scientist in September 2015. My buddy's wife agreed to let me live in their house, and it was only two miles from work.

It seemed like miracles followed me and Jeremy wherever we went, but the biggest miracle was the transformation that happened inside me. When I got back from Bahrain, I thought that building a relationship was one small part of a plan to keep me from sinking into ever deeper despair, but the more I shared myself with Jeremy, the more I realized that being in a fulfilling relationship was at the core of who I wanted to become.

Love wasn't just an emotion of excitement or the thrill of a new adventure; it was the realization of a dream that I had dreamt since I was a kid. When love called, it was the first time I responded for me: I'll go.

CPSIA information can be obtained
at www.ICGtesting.com
Printed in the USA
LVHW091339231120
672474LV00005B/20